Everyman's Poetry

Everyman, I will go with thee,
and be thy guide

William
Wordsworth

Selected and edited by STEPHEN LOGAN

University of Cambridge

EVERYMAN

J. M. Dent · London

This edition first published by Everyman Paperbacks in 1998
Selection, Introduction and other critical apparatus
© J. M. Dent 1998

Reprinted 2001, 2002, 2003, 2004

J. M. Dent
Orion Publishing Group
Orion House
5 Upper St Martin's Lane
London WC2H 9EA

Typeset by Deltatype Ltd, Birkenhead, Merseyside
Printed in Great Britain by
Clays Ltd, St Ives plc

British Library Cataloguing-in-Publication Data
is available on request

ISBN 0 460 87946 4

Contents

Note on the Author and Editor

WILLIAM WORDSWORTH was born on 7 April 1770. His background was comfortably middle-class; but the vicissitudes of his early life gave him a profound sympathy with the poor which governed his outlook and his poetry. One of five children, he developed an especially close relationship with his only sister, Dorothy. Following the death of his mother, he attended Hawkshead Grammar School, during which time his father died. In 1791, having obtained a mere pass degree from St John's College, Cambridge, he made his second trip to France. There he fell in love with Annette Vallon, the mother of his first child. Returning to England, he published his first substantial poems, *An Evening Walk* and *Descriptive Sketches*. A year later he nursed the dying Raisley Calvert, whose generous legacy in 1795 enabled Wordsworth to devote himself to poetry. Also in 1795, he met Coleridge, whose friendship profoundly nurtured his talent and resulted in the joint publication of *Lyrical Ballads* (1798). In 1802, he married a childhood friend, Mary Hutchinson, who bore him five children. The death at sea of his brother John in 1805 was the third in a long series of griefs which agitate his poems. In 1813 he was given a sinecure which relieved him of financial worry. During his middle years he was much involved in politics, local and national, which he treated as firmly subordinate to morality and religion. While producing many shorter poems, he was preoccupied with work on *The Recluse*, a gigantic poem, never finished, to which *The Prelude* was an introduction. In 1843 he was appointed Poet Laureate. He died in 1850, shortly before publication of *The Prelude*.

STEPHEN LOGAN is Lecturer in English at Magdalene College, Cambridge. He has completed a critical book, *The Estrangement of Wordsworth* and a collection of poems, *Heartlands*. He is now at work on an introduction to good reading, *Making Sense of Poems* and an accompanying annotated anthology, *The Critical Tradition*. He writes regularly on literary and cultural issues for the national press.

Chronology of Wordsworth's Life

Year	Age	Life
1770		Wordsworth born at Cockermouth, Lake District
1771	1	Only sister Dorothy born
1772	2	Favourite brother John born
1776–7	6–7	Attends nursery school in Penrith with Mary Hutchinson, his future wife
1778	8	Mother dies, aged 30
1783	13	Father dies, aged 42
1785	15	Writes first extant poem
1787	17	Enters St John's College, Cambridge
1788–9	18–19	Composes *An Evening Walk*
1790	20	Vacation spent walking in France and Switzerland
1791	21	B.A. without honours. Moves to London. Visits Wales; climbs Snowdon; leaves for France
1792	22	Meets Annette Vallon in Orleans; returns to London; Caroline, daughter by Annette born; *An Evening Walk* and *Descriptive Sketches* published; walks over Salisbury Plain; visits Tintern Abbey
1795	25	Raisley Calvert (brother of a Hawkshead schoolfriend) dies, leaving Wordsworth a legacy of £900; introduced to Godwin; meets Coleridge and Southey
1796	26	Spiritual crisis in which he yields up 'moral questions in despair'; begins his only play, *The Borderers*

Chronology of his Times

Year	Literary Context	Historical Events
1770		Beethoven born
1771	Scott born	
1772	Coleridge born	
1774	Southey born	
1775	Charles Lamb born	
1776	Adam Smith, *Wealth of Nations*	US Declaration of Independence
	Gibbon *Decline and Fall*	
1778	Hazlitt born	
1783		Pitt's first Ministry
1785	De Quincey born	
1788	Byron born	
1789	Blake, *Songs of Innocence*	French Revolution begins with Fall of Bastille
1791	Paine, *Rights of Man*	
	Boswell, *Life of Johnson*	
1792	Blake, *Marriage of Heaven and Hell*	France declares war on Austria and Prussia; Louis XVI imprisoned; September Massacres in Paris
	Shelley born	
1793	Godwin, *Political Justice*	Louis XVI executed; France declares war on England; Reign of Terror begins; Marie-Antoinette executed
1795	Keats born	
1796	Death of Burns	Napoleon's Italian campaign
	Coleridge, *Poems on Various Subjects*	

Year	Age	Life
1798	28	Describes scheme for *The Recluse*; *Lyrical Ballads* published; visits Germany; writes first lines of what became *The Prelude* and three Lucy poems
1799	29	Returns to England; completes *The Prelude* in its two-part version; settles with Dorothy at Dove Cottage, Grasmere
1801	31	Much-expanded edition of *Lyrical Ballads* published, with the famous Preface
1802	32	Visits Yorkshire, London, Dover and Calais where he spends a month with Annette; marries Mary Hutchinson; third edition of *Lyrical Ballads*
1803	33	Amid fears of French invasion, enlists in Westmorland Volunteers; son John born; tours Scotland; visits Burns's house and grave
1804	34	Expansion of *The Prelude* to five books; daughter Dora born
1805	35	Brother John drowned in Weymouth Bay; expansion of *The Prelude* to 13 books
1806	36	Son Thomas born; moves to a farmhouse in Coleorton, Leicester
1807	37	*Poems in Two Volumes* published; returns to Dove Cottage
1808	38	Completes *The White Doe of Rylstone*; moves to Allan Bank, Grasmere; Coleridge arrives and stays for two years; daughter Catharine born; De Quincey visits and stays
1809	39	Publishes disapproving pamphlet on The Convention of Cintra; part of *Reply to Mathetes* appears in *The Friend*
1810	40	Conclusion of *Reply to Mathetes*; son William born; estrangement from Coleridge

Year	Literary Context	Historical Events
1797	Coleridge writes *Kubla Khan* and first version of *The Ancient Mariner* Death of Burke	
1798	Coleridge, *Fears in Solitude*	Irish Rebellion
1799	Royal Institution founded	November: Napoleon made First Consul
1801	Southey, *Thalaba*	Addington's Ministry replaces Pitt's
1802	Coleridge, first version of 'Dejection: an Ode'	Treaty of Amiens; temporary peace between England and France; war with France resumed
1803	Coleridge, *Poems*	
1804	Blake completes *Milton* Death of Kant	Napoleon becomes Emperor, Addington Ministry collapses; 2nd Pitt Ministry begins; Spain declares war on Britain
1805	Scott, *Lay of the Last Minstrel*	Battle of Trafalgar
1806		Death of Fox and Pitt
1807		Abolition of Slave Trade
1808	Goethe, *Faust*, Part I Scott, *Marmion* *The Examiner* begins *Quarterly Review* founded	Convention of Cintra
1809	Coleridge first issues *The Friend*	Perceval Ministry
1810	Blake working on *Jerusalem* and *Vala* Coleridge, *The Friend* ceases publication	1st Reform Bill since 1797; George III officially acknowledged insane

Year	Age	Life
1811	41	Moves to The Rectory, Grasmere; teaches briefly at Grasmere school
1812	42	Partial reconciliation with Coleridge; daughter Catharine dies; son Thomas dies
1813	43	Appointed Distributor of Stamps for Westmorland; moves to Rydal Mount, between Grasmere and Ambleside
1814	44	Tours Scotland; *The Excursion* published
1815	45	Collected (shorter) *Poems* published; *The White Doe of Rylstone* published
1817	47	Meets Keats at Haydon's house, London
1819	49	Begins major revision of *The Prelude*; appointed J.P.; *Peter Bell* published; *Vaudracour and Julia* (fictionalized account of affair with Annette) extracted from *The Prelude* and published; tours Continent; in Paris meets Annette; four-volume *Miscellaneous* [collected] *Poems* published
1822	52	*A Description of the Scenery of the Lakes* published
1827	57	Five-volume *Poetical Works* (third collected edition)
1831	61	Last meetings with Coleridge; visits Scott at Abbotsford; tours Highlands
1832	62	Second major revision of *The Prelude*; four-volume *Poetical Works* (fourth collected edition) published
1835	65	*Yarrow Revisited and Other Poems* published; writes 'Extempore Effusion'
1836–7	66–7	Six-volume *Poetical Works* (fifth collected edition) published

Year	Literary Context	Historical Events
1811	Shelley, *The Necessity of Atheism* Austen, *Sense and Sensibility*	Prince of Wales made Regent
1812	Byron, *Childe Harold*, I–II	Napoleon invades Russia; Retreat from Moscow; US declares war on Britain
1813	Byron, *The Giaour* Austen, *Pride and Prejudice*	Leigh Hunt imprisoned for libelling Prince Regent
1814	Scott, *Waverley* Austen, *Mansfield Park*	Napoleon exiled to Elba; Congress of Vienna
1815	Scott, *Guy Mannering*	Battle of Waterloo; end of Napoleonic Wars
1816	Austen, *Emma*	
1817	Coleridge, *Biographia Literaria* Keats, *Poems*	
1821	Death of Keats De Quincey, *Confessions of an English Opium Eater*	
1822	Death of Shelley	Coronation of George IV
1827	Death of Blake	Death of Beethoven
1831	J. S. Mill, 'The Spirit of the Age'	
1832	Death of Scott, Crabbe and Goethe	Reform Bill passed
1834	Death of Coleridge Death of Lamb	Poor Law Amendment Act

Year	Age	Life
1837	67	Last Continental tour, visits Rome and Venice
1838	68	One-volume edition of his sonnets published; third major revision of *The Prelude*; campaigns for authors' copyright
1839	69	Receives honorary doctorate from Oxford University
1841	71	Annette Yallon dies. Dora Wordsworth marries Edward Quillinan
1842	72	*Poems Chiefly of Early and Late Years* published; resigns Distributorship of Stamps and receives Civil List pension of £300 a year
1843	73	Succeeds Southey as Poet Laureate
1845	75	Meets Tennyson; one-volume *Poems* (sixth collected edition) published
1847		Dora Wordsworth dies, aged 42
1849–50	79–80	Six-volume *Poetical Works* (seventh collected edition) published
1850	80	Death of Wordsworth; *The Prelude* published

Year	Literary Context	Historical Events
1837	Dickens, *Pickwick Papers*	Accession of Victoria
1838	Dickens, *Oliver Twist*	Chartists demand suffrage
1839	Dickens, *Nicholas Nickleby*	Copyright Bill passed
1841	Carlyle, *On Heroes and Hero Worship*	Peel becomes Prime Minister
1842	Tennyson, *Poems*	Chartist agitation
1843	Dickens *A Christmas Carol* Southey dies	
1845	Disraeli, *Sybil*	Newman received into Roman Catholic Church
1847	Anne Brontë, *Agnes Grey* Charlotte Brontë, *Jane Eyre* Emily Brontë, *Wuthering Heights*	
1848	Thackeray, *Vanity fair*	
1849	Coleridge, *Notes and Lectures on Shakespeare*	
1850	Tennyson, *In Memoriam*	

Introduction

Wordsworth was the longest-lived of the great English Romantic poets. This simple fact has a number of important implications. First, he wrote a great deal. Second, he had time to revise his poems extensively. Third, he experienced and contributed to deep changes of society and culture. These changes are reflected in his poems and in the changing attitudes towards them.

Wordsworth was thirty before the eighteenth century ended; he was fourteen before Samuel Johnson (1709–84), the chief proponent of English Augustanism, died. Hence Augustanism was for Wordsworth (as it was not for Keats [1795–1821]) the prevailing outlook among the adults he grew up with. Wordsworth once said that his prose was too formal and elaborate because he'd never outgrown the influence of a schoolmaster who admired Johnson's neo-classical grandeur. Augustanism, roughly speaking, was an attempt to promote in English literature and society the values thought characteristic of classical Greece and Rome. In poetry, this meant elegance and succinctness of expression, accompanied by emotional restraint, all in the service of a system of moral values refined through tradition and aligned with Christianity.

It was in this cultural climate that the young Wordsworth began developing his own distinctive outlook and made his first attempts at poetry. There were aspects of Augustanism that Wordsworth liked; others he loathed. He liked its principled conservatism, but loathed its complicity with social injustice. The principal source of the nervous breakdown he suffered in 1796 was a conflict between the wish to promote good political change and a wish to conserve equally good moral traditions. In 1793 he wrote a denunciation of the Bishop of Llandaff's apparent indifference to the poor. This was not an attack on Christianity, since concern for the poor is a duty enjoined no less by Christ than by Wordsworth; but it *was* an attack on the tendency of institutions (here the church) to cramp 'the human heart by which we live'.[1] Just five years later, however,

[1] Ode ['Intimations of Immortality'], 1. 203.

Wordsworth wrote in the Advertisement to *Lyrical Ballads* (1798) that it was only by long continued study of 'the best models' that readers could hope to acquire 'an accurate taste in poetry'— an opinion which most Augustan writers would have endorsed.

Wordsworth is at once the most revolutionary, and the most conservative of the great English Romantics, possibly of all English poets. He would, I suspect, have agreed with T. S. Eliot's dictum that sometimes it is more distinguished 'to be original with the *minimum* of alteration' than 'with the *maximum* . . .'. And he was, equally probably, foremost of the poets whom Eliot had in mind when he declared that 'sensibility alters from generation to generation in everybody, whether we will or no; but expression is only altered by a man of genius.'[1]

What Eliot's dictum, applied to Wordsworth, would mean is that Wordsworth re-established the relation between poetry and speech. This is important because it is in speech that the current sensibility — the whole interlocking system of habits of thinking and feeling — is embodied. The last great poet before Wordsworth was Pope (1688–1744). In the fifty years between Pope's death and Wordsworth's reaching poetic maturity in the late 1790s, poets had, for the most part, continued to write in Pope's manner. That is to say, in the overtly ingenious, antithetical manner which became synonymous with the heroic couplet. But sensibility had, inexorably, moved on, so that a gap was evident between what Wordsworth denounced as 'the gaudiness and inane phraseology'[2] of much poetry and the way that people were actually thinking, feeling and speaking.

Wordsworth believed that the speech most perfectly attuned to 'the essential passions of the heart'[3] was not that of educated people living in cities, but of people living in constant communication with the grand and enduring objects of nature. His theory, expressed in the famous Preface to *Lyrical Ballads* (1800), was that God had so created human beings that their most important feelings would be stirred by beautiful scenery, thus keeping them emotionally alive and healthy. Hence it was to people living amid such scenery that poets should look for the language in which to

---

[1] Both quotations are from Eliot's introduction (1930) to Johnson's *London* and *The Vanity of Human Wishes*.

[2] Advertisement to *Lyrical Ballads* (1798).

[3] Preface to *Lyrical Ballads* (1800).

express their deepest feelings. Wordsworth himself sought 'a selection of the real language of men in a state of vivid sensation.'[1] In a note to 'The Thorn' — a poem which contains some of his most defiantly humdrum phrasing — Wordsworth asserts that the language of deepest passion is characterized by simple words and repetition, such as we find in the Authorized Version of the Bible. The aim of using such language was to achieve 'the unostentatious beauties of a pure style'[2] — an aim which, as the ambiguity of 'pure' suggests, was at once aesthetic and moral.

Following Eliot, F. R. Leavis affirmed in some notes found after his death that Wordsworth was the poet of genius who 'altered expression'. Yet he is also, Leavis rightly perceived, the most neglected of the great English poets. Why should this be? According to such influential commentators, Wordsworth effected a permanent change in the way poets write, making it possible both to express and to rouse into health-giving action, the profoundest human emotions. So why should he now, despite signs of a resurgence of interest in him among living poets such as Seamus Heaney and R. S. Thomas, be so under-appreciated?

The reason is, I believe, that the complex system of cultural changes which he helped instigate, has estranged us from many of the basic presuppositions which inform his poetry. When we bump into these beliefs therefore — often without being consciously aware of it — we are either repelled by them, or don't recognize them for what they are, or else we pretend they are something else.

The view that Wordsworth had two voices — serious and namby-pamby — was established as early as Byron's review of *Poems in Two Volumes* (1807). Modern criticism, accepting this, has tended to focus on the serious, quasi-philosophical poetry to the exclusion of the gentler poems represented in Palgrave's *Golden Treasury* (1861), where Wordsworth has the greatest number of poems after Shakespeare. There is need for a reconciliation between ourselves and Wordsworth and thus between the gentler and the severer aspects of his achievement. This is unlikely to occur until it is recognized a) that Wordsworth was throughout his career a Christian poet; b) that he considered himself primarily a teacher; and c) that his slightest lyrics are no less 'philosophical' (in his sense of being concerned with wisdom) than his loftiest blank verse.

---

[1] Preface to *Lyrical Ballads*.
[2] Essay, Supplementary to the Preface to *Poems* (1815).

For example, in 'Tintern Abbey' we get a characteristically unobtrusive insistence on the paradox that pleasure can be disturbing:

> And I have felt
> A pleasure that disturbs me with the joy
> Of elevated thoughts . . .[1]

This is perhaps to be expected in a poem which is obviously concerned to register both the grandeur and the distinctiveness of Wordsworth's experience of God in the world. Yet he alludes to a similar contrariety at the start of the first of his three poems 'On the Daisy':[2]

> In youth from rock to rock I went,
> From hill to hill, in discontent
> Of pleasure high and turbulent,
> Most pleas'd when most uneasy . . .

Moreover, in our predilection for the Shakespearian virtues of 'sensuous particularity', indirectness, and density of meaning, we are apt to discount Wordsworth's right, both in his meditative blank verse and in his shorter poems to be more prosaically direct and hortatory. The slight lyric, 'Yes! thou art fair . . .', might (justly) be thought less profound than 'Elegiac Stanzas' in its treatment of the theme of the mind's creativity in perception. Yet it achieves, by virtue of its very simplicity, a sternly gallant jauntiness of manner which it is touching to see Wordsworth assume in his 76th year. Similarly, though the 'spots of time' episodes in *The Prelude* will be remembered chiefly for their singular depth of implication, we owe the phrase by which we designate them to a stretch of more prosaic verse in between the narratives.[3]

The ablest Romantic and Victorian readers valued Wordsworth's poetry equally for its artistry and its import: they wanted to learn what Wordsworth had to teach and therefore did not need to make

---

[1] L. 94–6. Compare 'Not undisturbed by the delight it feels' (A Night-Piece', l.24) and 'Nutting', esp. ll. 37–51.

[2] Wordsworth and Coleridge frequently referred to the language of poetry as being, at its best, 'philosophical': i.e., morally and psychologically accurate. Hence Wordsworth's rebuke to someone who mentioned this poem as being on '*a* daisy'. He corrected them, saying that it was on '*the* daisy, a mighty difference!' (like that between 'a' and 'the' human heart).

[3] 1805, xi. 257–72.

a false distinction between the aesthetic and the admonitory elements in Wordsworth's poetic character. Our own situation is different.

Perhaps the single most important thing to remember when reading Wordsworth is that we are post-Romantics. This means both that we derive many of our ideas about art from the Romantics; and also that our cultural milieu is in certain crucial respects unlike theirs. We are too often beguiled by the similarities into ignoring, or underestimating, the differences of outlook. This strange blend of likeness to and difference from ourselves is evident not only in Wordsworth's general statements but in minute details of style.

Victorian critics, writing before the onset of Modernism and the dissolution of cultural traditions which formerly stretched unbroken across post-medieval literature, could count on a degree of cultural affinity with Wordsworth which no longer exists. Thus Matthew Arnold, being culturally in sympathy with Wordsworth, could write in 1879: 'He has no style' without supposing he would be taken to mean that Wordsworth was careless about his style. Not until A. C. Bradley in 1909 did it seem necessary to point out the danger of this way of speaking. Hopkins and Clough were also duly attentive to the blend of perfection and imperfection in Wordsworth, while yet revering him as a master, both morally and stylistically. As so often, it is Coleridge who strikes the right critical note with his ascription to Wordsworth of a 'curiosa felicitas' or studied felicity of expression, such as *'chiming* hounds' in 'Simon Lee' — apt, because to Simon, the hounds' 'voices' were sweet as a bell. Yet Wordsworth's self-effacing artistry in such details is no less a feat of moral insight.

It might be thought, given his pro-democratic sympathies and his early dream of having his poems published in a form which could be sold cheap by pedlars, that Wordsworth shared the current view of poetry as an art which anyone can gain access to. But he was a learned and scrupulous craftsman, very insistent on the importance of 'workmanship' and study: 'my poems must be much more nearly looked at before they can give rise to any remarks of much value, even from the strongest minds.'[1] Moreover, workmanship for him was a moral issue. Hence his disparagement

---

[1] Letter to Sir George Beaumont, February 1808.

of Byron and his insistence on the need for long study of best masters. In 1815 he reaffirmed his long-standing view that it was only those who had made a *study* of poetry whose judgment of it could be trusted.[1]

Among the general issues by which the character of a poet's style is conditioned, religion is the one where the clearest differences between ourselves and Wordsworth emerge. For example, Aldous Huxley (whose grandfather apparently coined the term 'agnostic') claims that Wordsworth pumped the landscape full of Anglicanism.[2] This is a judgment whose recklessness would not have gone undetected in an age less indifferent, or hostile, to formal religion than our own. For one thing I doubt whether Huxley was distinguishing carefully between Anglicanism and other forms of Christianity. Most of Wordsworth's critics, prior to Modernism, had been Christians; and their complaints that Wordsworth was too vague about matters of doctrine could hardly have been made if they'd been thinking in terms as approximate as Huxley's. Further, Huxley would presumably not have objected to Wordsworth's filling the landscape with secular humanism. There is a world of difference between leaning towards agnosticism from a standpoint of Christian faith, and peering towards agnosticism through a fog of unbelief.

Wordsworth had a low opinion of formal philosophy, which in any case scarcely existed as an academic discipline in late eighteenth century England. Philosophy for him was more a matter of an enlightened outlook on life; and the value to him of poetry was that it could communicate this with unrivalled force. He wished, he said (in words we should weigh), 'to be considered as a Teacher, or as nothing.'[3] Dry ethical discussions, of the sort he had once admired in Godwin's book *Political Justice* (1793), were, he came to realize, powerless to 'melt into our affections.'[4] It was Wordsworth's skill in imparting the essence of his outlook by exploiting the expressive powers peculiar to poetry that inspired Shelley's remark that 'the imagination is the prime agent of morality and poetry ministers to the effect by operating upon the cause.'

It is pretty certain that Wordsworth would have had little patience with the majority of modern academic studies of his work,

[1] Essay, Supplementary to the Preface to *Poems* (1815).
[2] 'Wordsworth in the Tropics', from *Do What You Will* (1931).
[3] Letter to Sir George Beaumont.
[4] 'Essay on Morals' (1798).

which too rarely ask the question why his poetry really matters and whose writers seem so little prepared to learn anything from him. The comparative neglect of Wordsworth's lyrics is not the result of critical discrimination, but of a preference for verse which, being more openly discursive and less openly Christian, is more amenable to current styles of critical discourse. As Wordsworth said himself, the praise he wanted most was that of people whose suffering he had helped to lighten. Among those of his contemporaries whose opinions he valued, his death was lamented in grief-stricken terms:

> Time may restore us in his course
> Goethe's sage mind and Byron's force;
> But where will Europe's latter hour
> Again find Wordsworth's healing power?[1]

Wordsworth believed a poet should help 'render [our] feelings more sane, pure and permanent.'[2] He claimed that there was

> . . . scarcely one of my Poems which does not aim to direct the attention to some moral sentiment, or to some general principle, or law of thought, or of our intellectual constitution.[3]

This was recognized and appreciated by contemporaries such as Coleridge, Lamb and De Quincey. Equally, it was recognized by such Victorians as John Stuart Mill and Mark Rutherford — both of whom credited Wordsworth with helping them to survive profound spiritual crises — and by Matthew Arnold, whose term *healing power* most aptly describes this central aspect of Wordsworth's poetic character.

Modern readers, particularly those influenced by modern academic criticism (which often dismisses the past as a graveyard of discredited 'ideologies') may be inclined to think of Wordsworth's healing power as merely a historical phenomenon, available to Romantics and Victorians, but not to us. This, in my opinion, is a mistake. We have only to ask what Wordsworth's healing power was, and why it was so warmly appreciated, in order to perceive its continuing relevance to ourselves.

Wordsworth was born in the immediate aftermath of what is

[1] Matthew Arnold, 'Memorial Verses' (1850), ll. 60–3.
[2] Letter to John Wilson, June 1802.
[3] Letter to Lady Beaumont, 21 May 1807.

conventionally, and somewhat unaptly, known as the Enlighten-
ment: the era in European history when influential thinkers began
to subject even the most sacrosanct traditional beliefs to intellectual
scrutiny. This led to an over-reliance on discursive (as distinct from
intuitive) reasoning which Wordsworth explicitly opposed.[1] More-
over, the Enlightenment marked the beginning of a process which
led to modern relativism, or the belief that morality is the product of
social conditioning and has no ultimate sanction.

Wordsworth saw this development coming. He was far from
sharing the modern indifference to Christianity and what Coleridge
called 'the eternal Verities of Plato and Descartes'. Concentrating
on 'the great and universal passions of men',[2] he struggled to
reaffirm through poetry the grounds for believing that 'we have all
of us one human heart'.[3] His poetry registers the distress which
many of us feel at the slippage of those certainties traditionally felt
to be necessary to a healthy, humane existence; but more than
that, it shows him overcoming this distress in a strong recognition
of the values by which all human beings — regardless of
differences of culture, class and creed — are in fact united.
Wordsworth's healing power, therefore, consists in his ability to
provide, by means of his poetic art, moral reassurances which, deep
down, we crave. And perhaps we need this power the more acutely
because the temptations to moral despair are greater now than ever
before.

STEPHEN LOGAN

[1] See 'Expostulation and Reply', 'The Tables Turned' and the passage from *The
Prelude* below entitled 'Blessed the Infant Babe'.
[2] Preface to *Lyrical Ballads*.
[3] 'The Old Cumberland Beggar', l. 146.

Note on The Text

Arrangement of Poems   The division of the selected poems into those published during and after Wordsworth's lifetime is the result of my wish to redress two kinds of imbalance. Owing to the immensely valuable recent work of scholars in editing his manuscripts, there has been a tendency to value poems which he did not publish at the expense of those he did. For example, the poems now known as 'The Ruined Cottage', and 'The Pedlar' were never published by Wordsworth in their current forms (though he did at various times think of them as independent poems). Then there is the very different, yet related case, of *The Prelude*, now familiar to many readers in three versions (1799, 1805, 1850), yet which Wordsworth himself did not publish. Nonetheless, a cursory examination of Wordsworth criticism over the past thirty years would reveal a far more intense preoccupation with these poems, and with the projected *The Recluse* than with either his lyrics, or the one substantial part of *The Recluse* which he *did* publish, namely *The Excursion*. Consequently, I have devoted most of my allotted pages to poems published in Wordsworth's lifetime and have given them in the versions (subsequently much revised) in which they made their first impact on the public. The relegation of *The Prelude* to the class of unpublished poems is meant less to downgrade that poem than to upgrade others which Wordsworth was less hesitant about, and which his first few generations of readers knew better.

Choice of Poems   While not sharing Matthew Arnold's low opinion of *The Prelude*, I have reverted a little towards him in giving priority to the shorter poems. Owing to the disproportionate attention bestowed on *The Prelude*, the lyrics have in recent years suffered neglect. Also, since *The Prelude* was never published— apart from a few excerpts[1]— in Wordsworth's lifetime, his reputation was established independently of it. Alongside the poems that Wordsworth enthusiasts would expect to see, I have added a sprinkling of poems published in Wordsworth's lifetime but

[1] 'There was a Boy', 'The Influence of Natural Objects' and 'The Simplon Pass'.

not currently as well known. Square brackets round a poem's title indicate that it was untitled when originally published.

For poems published in Wordsworth's lifetime I have used the first published texts. For poems published from manuscripts, I have used the first stable text, as far as this can be determined. For *The Prelude* I have used the text of 1805 on the grounds that: a) this was the version of the rapidly-evolving text which remained stable longest and was considered complete by Coleridge, to whom the poem had been shown or read at each stage of its composition; b) those extracts from *The Prelude* published in Wordsworth's lifetime were taken from a version close to this one; c) the first published text (1850) did not appear in Wordsworth's lifetime either, so it is on a similar footing to the other versions; d) it appears to have been autobiographical scruple and the wish to complete *The Recluse* that prevented Wordsworth from publishing the 1805 text.

Extracts from Wordsworth's own writings are accompanied by their dates of publication. Extracts from the notes Wordsworth dictated to his friend Isabella Fenwick in 1842–3 are dated '1843'. Versions of *The Prelude* are cited as 1799, 1805 or 1850. Dates of composition and publication, where known, are given after the poem, the former in the left-hand margin, the latter in the right.

Acknowledgements

I should like to express my thanks to the editors of The Cornell Wordsworth, particularly James Butler, Karen Green, Jared Curtis and Mark Reed; also to John O. Hayden, Michael Mason, Jonathan Wordsworth and Stephen Gill.

William Wordsworth

Old Man Travelling;

Animal Tranquillity and Decay, a Sketch[1]

   The little hedge-row birds,
That peck along the road, regard him not.
He travels on,[2] and in his face, his step,
His gait, is one expression; every limb,
His look and bending figure, all bespeak   5
A man who does not move with pain, but moves
With thought—He is insensibly subdued
To settled quiet: he is one by whom
All effort seems forgotten, one to whom
Long patience has such mild composure given,   10
That patience now doth seem a thing, of which
He hath no need. He is by nature led
To peace so perfect, that the young behold
With envy, what the old man hardly feels.
—I asked him whither he was bound, and what 15
The object of his journey; he replied
'Sir! I am going many miles to take
'A last leave of my son, a mariner,
'Who from a sea-fight has been brought to Falmouth,[3]
'And there is dying in an hospital.'   20

1796   1798

[1] 'Animal' could mean either 'spiritual' (from Latin *anima*, soul) or 'bodily'.
If the former, then 'Animal' applies only to 'Tranquillity': if the latter, it
applies also to 'Decay'.
[2] Cp. 'The Old Cumberland Beggar', ll. 24 and 44.
[3] A Cornish port near the extreme south-west tip of England.

Lines Left upon a Seat in a Yew-tree which stands near the lake of Esthwaite, on a desolate part of the shore, yet commanding a beautiful prospect

– Nay, Traveller! rest. This lonely yew-tree stands
Far from all human dwelling: what if here
No sparkling rivulet spread[1] the verdant herb;
What if these barren boughs the bee not loves;
Yet, if the wind breathe soft, the curling waves,   5
That break against the shore, shall lull thy mind
By one soft impulse saved from vacancy.

——————Who he was[2]
That piled these stones, and with the mossy sod
First covered o'er, and taught this aged tree,   10
Now wild, to bend its arms in circling shade,
I well remember.—He was one who own'd
No common soul. In youth, by genius nurs'd,
And big with lofty views, he to the world
Went forth, pure in his heart, against the taint   15
Of dissolute tongues, 'gainst jealousy, and hate,
And scorn, against all enemies prepared,
All but neglect: and so, his spirit damped
At once, with rash disdain he turned away,
And with the food of pride sustained his soul   20
In solitude.—Stranger! these gloomy boughs
Had charms for him; and here he loved to sit,
His only visitants a straggling sheep,
The stone-chat, or the glancing sand-piper;
And on these barren rocks, with juniper,   25
And heath, and thistle, thinly sprinkled o'er,
Fixing his downward eye, he many an hour

---

[1] '(Should) spread over' and/or 'should propagate'.
[2] The character of the recluse is believed to be loosely based on a Rev. William Braithwaite of Satterhow, who, like Wordsworth, attended Hawkshead Grammar School and St John's College. Cambridge.

A morbid pleasure nourished, tracing here
An emblem of his own unfruitful life:
And lifting up his head, he then would gaze   30
On the more distant scene; how lovely 'tis
Thou seest, and he would gaze till it became
Far lovelier, and his heart could not sustain
The beauty still more beauteous. Nor, that time,
Would he forget those beings, to whose minds,   35
Warm from the labours of benevolence,
The world, and man himself, appeared a scene
Of kindred loveliness: then he would sigh
With mournful joy, to think that others felt
What he must never feel: and so, lost man!   40
On visionary views[1] would fancy feed,
Till his eye streamed with tears. In this deep vale
He died, this seat his only monument.

If thou be one whose heart the holy forms
Of young imagination have kept pure,   45
Stranger! henceforth be warned; and know, that pride,
Howe'er disguised in its own majesty,
Is littleness; that he, who feels contempt
For any living thing, hath faculties
Which he has never used; that thought with him   50
Is in its infancy. The man, whose eye
Is ever on himself, doth look on one,
The least of nature's works, one who might move
The wise man to that scorn which wisdom holds
Unlawful, ever. O, be wiser thou!   55
Instructed that true knowledge leads to love,
True dignity abides with him alone
Who, in the silent hour of inward thought,
Can still suspect, and still revere himself,
In lowliness of heart.   60

1797   1798

[1] 'Mystical imaginings' and/or 'impractical ideas'.

The Old Cumberland Beggar, a Description

The class of Beggars to which the old man here described belongs, will probably soon be extinct. It consists of poor, and, mostly, old and infirm persons, who confined themselves to a stated round in their neighbourhood, and had certain fixed days, on which, at different houses, they regularly received charity; sometimes in money, but mostly in provisions.[1]

I saw an aged Beggar in my walk,
And he was seated by the highway side,
On a low structure of rude masonry
Built at the foot of a huge hill, that they
Who lead their horses down the steep rough road   5
May thence remount at ease. The aged Man
Had placed his staff across the broad smooth stone
That overlays the pile, and, from a bag
All white with flour the dole of village dames,
He drew his scraps and fragments, one by one;   10
And scanned them with a fix'd and serious look
Of idle computation. In the sun,
Upon the second step of that small pile,
Surrounded by those wild unpeopled hills,
He sate,[2] and ate his food in solitude;   15
And ever, scatter'd from his palsied hand,
That still attempting to prevent the waste,
Was baffled still, the crumbs in little showers
Fell on the ground; and the small mountain birds
Not venturing yet to peck their destin'd meal,   20
Approached within the length of half his staff.
Him from my childhood have I known, and then
He was so old, he seems not older now;
He travels on, a solitary man,
So helpless in appearance, that for him   25
The sauntering horseman-traveller does not throw
With careless hand his alms upon the ground,
But stops, that he may safely lodge the coin
Within the old Man's hat; nor quits him so,
But still when he has given his horse the rein   30

---

[1] Wordsworth's headnote (1800).
[2] Archaic past-tense of 'sit', changed to 'sat' in 1805.

Towards the aged Beggar turns a look,
Sidelong and half-reverted. She who tends
The toll-gate, when in summer at her door
She turns her wheel, if on the road she sees
The aged Beggar coming, quits her work,   35
And lifts the latch for him that he may pass.
The Post-boy when his rattling wheels o'ertake
The aged Beggar, in the woody lane,
Shouts to him from behind, and, if perchance
The old Man does not change his course, the Boy   40
Turns with less noisy wheels to the road-side,
And passes gently by, without a curse
Upon his lips, or anger at his heart.
He travels on, a solitary Man,
His age has no companion. On the ground   45
His eyes are turn'd, and, as he moves along,
They move along the ground; and evermore,
Instead of common and habitual sight
Of fields with rural works, of hill and dale,
And the blue sky, one little span of earth   50
Is all his prospect. Thus, from day to day,
Bowbent,[1] his eyes for ever on the ground,
He plies his weary journey, seeing still,
And never knowing that he sees, some straw,
Some scatter'd leaf, or marks which, in one track,   55
The nails of cart or chariot[2] wheel have left
Impress'd on the white road, in the same line,
At distance still the same. Poor Traveller!
His staff trails with him, scarcely do his feet
Disturb the summer dust, he is so still   60
In look and motion, that the cottage curs,
Ere he have pass'd the door, will turn away
Weary of barking at him. Boys and girls,
The vacant and the busy, maids and youths,
And urchins newly breech'd—all pass him by: 65
Him even the slow-pac'd waggon leaves behind.

But deem not this Man useless. —— Statesmen! ye

[1] 'Bent like a bow.'
[2] In the 18th and 19th centuries, a light, open, horse-drawn carriage.

Who are so restless in your wisdom, ye
Who have a broom still ready in your hands
To rid the world of nuisances; ye proud,   70
Heart-swoln, while in your pride ye contemplate
Your talents, power, and wisdom, deem him not
A burthen of the earth. 'Tis Nature's[1] law
That none, the meanest of created things,
Of forms created the most vile and brute,   75
The dullest or most noxious, should exist
Divorced from good, a spirit and pulse of good,
A life and soul to every mode of being
Inseparably link'd. While thus he creeps
From door to door, the Villagers in him   80
Behold a record which together binds
Past deeds and offices of charity
Else unremember'd, and so keeps alive
The kindly mood in hearts which lapse of years,
And that half-wisdom half-experience gives   85
Make slow to feel, and by sure steps resign
To selfishness and cold oblivious cares.
Among the farms and solitary huts,
Hamlets, and thinly-scattered villages,
Where'er the aged Beggar takes his rounds,   90
The mild necessity of use[2] compels
To acts of love; and habit does the work
Of reason, yet prepares that after-joy
Which reason cherishes. And thus the soul,
By that sweet taste of pleasure unpursu'd   95
Doth find itself insensibly dispos'd
To virtue and true goodness. Some there are,
By their good works exalted, lofty minds
And meditative, authors of delight
And happiness, which to the end of time   100
Will live, and spread, and kindle; minds like these,
In childhood, from this solitary being,
This helpless wanderer, have perchance receiv'd,
(A thing more precious far than all that books
Or the solicitudes of love can do!)   105

[1] 'Nature' here means 'the whole of the perceptible created universe'.
[2] Custom: the state of being used to doing something.

That first mild touch of sympathy and thought,
In which they found their kindred with a world
Where want and sorrow were. The easy man[1]
Who sits at his own door,—and, like the pear
Which overhangs his head from the green wall,   110
Feeds in the sunshine; the robust and young,
The prosperous and unthinking, they who live
Shelter'd, and flourish in a little grove
Of their own kindred, all behold in him
A silent monitor,[2] which on their minds   115
Must needs impress a transitory thought
Of self-congratulation, to the heart
Of each recalling his peculiar boons,
His charters and exemptions; and, perchance,
Though he to no one give the fortitude   120
And circumspection needful to preserve
His present blessings, and to husband up
The respite of the season, he, at least,
And 'tis no vulgar service, makes them felt.

Yet further.—Many, I believe, there are   125
Who live a life of virtuous decency,
Men who can hear the Decalogue[3] and feel
No self-reproach, who of the moral law[4]
Establish'd in the land where they abide
Are strict observers, and not negligent,   130
Meanwhile, in any tenderness of heart
Or act of love to those with whom they dwell,
Their kindred, and the children of their blood.
Praise be to such, and to their slumbers peace!
— But of the poor man ask, the abject poor,   135
Go, and demand of him, if there be here,
In this cold abstinence from evil deeds,
And these inevitable charities,
Wherewith to satisfy the human soul.

[1] 'comfortable (financially and hence physically)'.
[2] 'reminder or warning'.
[3] The Ten Commandments (Exodus. 20:1–17).
[4] A philosophical term deriving from St Paul (Romans 2:14–15) and meaning 'the system of intuitable moral norms'.

No—man is dear to man: the poorest poor   140
Long for some moments in a weary life
When they can know and feel that they have been
Themselves the fathers and the dealers out
Of some small blessings, have been kind to such
As needed kindness, for this single cause,   145
That we have all of us one human heart.
—Such pleasure is to one kind Being known,
My Neighbour, when with punctual care, each week
Duly as Friday comes, though press'd herself
By her own wants, she from her chest[1] of meal   150
Takes one unsparing handful for the scrip[2]
Of this old Mendicant, and, from her door
Returning with exhilarated heart,
Sits by her fire, and builds her hope in heav'n.

Then let him pass, a blessing on his head!   155
And while, in that vast solitude to which
The tide of things has led him, he appears
To breathe and live but for himself alone,
Unblam'd, uninjur'd, let him bear about
The good which the benignant law of heaven   160
Has hung around him, and, while life is his,
Still let him prompt the unletter'd Villagers
To tender offices and pensive thoughts.
Then let him pass, a blessing on his head!
And, long as he can wander, let him breathe   165
The freshness of the vallies, let his blood
Struggle with frosty air and winter snows,
And let the charter'd[3] wind that sweeps the heath
Beat his grey locks against his wither'd face.
Reverence the hope whose vital anxiousness   170
Gives the last human interest to his heart.
May never House, misnamed of industry,[4]
Make him a captive; for that pent-up din,

[1] Storage-box.
[2] Knapsack: specifically of the kind once associated with pilgrims.
[3] 'licensed (to roam freely)'.
[4] The workhouse, where work was meant to be provided for able-bodied paupers in return for food and lodging paid for out of local parish funds.

Those life-consuming sounds that clog the air,
Be his the natural silence of old age.   175
Let him be free of[1] mountain solitudes,
And have around him, whether heard or not,
The pleasant melody of woodland birds.
Few are his pleasures; if his eyes, which now
Have been so long familiar with the earth,   180
No more behold the horizontal sun,
Rising or setting, let the light at least
Find a free entrance to their languid orbs.
And let him, *where* and *when* he will, sit down
Beneath the trees, or by the grassy bank   185
Of high-way side, and with the little birds
Share his chance-gather'd meal, and, finally,
As in the eye of Nature he has liv'd,
So in the eye of Nature let him die.

1796–8   1800

We Are Seven

A simple child, dear brother Jim,[2]
That lightly draws its breath,
And feels its life in every limb,
What should it know of death?

I met a little cottage girl,   5
She was eight years old, she said;
Her hair was thick with many a curl
That cluster'd round her head.

She had a rustic, woodland air,
And she was wildly clad;   10

[1] 'allowed to enjoy or make use of'.
[2] In 1843 Wordsworth said that the first stanza was composed extempore
by Coleridge.

Her eyes were fair, and very fair,
—Her beauty made me glad.

'Sisters and brothers, little maid,
'How many may you be?'
'How many? seven in all,' she said,   15
And wondering looked at me.

'And where are they, I pray you tell?'
She answered, 'Seven are we,
'And two of us at Conway¹ dwell,
'And two are gone to sea.   20

'Two of us in the church-yard lie,
'My sister and my brother,
'And in the church-yard cottage, I
'Dwell near them with my mother.'

'You say that two at Conway dwell   25
'And two are gone to sea,
'Yet you are seven; I pray you tell
'Sweet Maid, how this may be?'

Then did the little Maid reply,
'Seven boys and girls are we;   30
'Two of us in the church-yard lie,
'Beneath the church-yard tree.'

'You run about, my little maid,
'Your limbs they are alive;
'If two are in the church-yard laid,   35
'Then ye² are only five.'

'Their graves are green, they may be seen,'
The little Maid replied,
'Twelve steps or more from my mother's door,
'And they are side by side.   40

¹ A market-town near the coast in North Wales.
² The shift from 'you' to 'ye' suggests an increase of tenderness, probably
from its use in dialects as a friendly alternative to the more formal 'you'.

'My stockings there I often knit,
'My 'kerchief[1] there I hem;
'And there upon the ground I sit—
'I sit and sing to them.

'And often after sunset, Sir,[2]   45
'When it is light and fair,
'I take my little porringer,[3]
'And eat my supper there.

'The first that died was little Jane;
'In bed she moaning lay,   50
'Till God released her of[4] her pain,
'And then she went away.

'So in the church-yard she was laid,
'And all the summer dry,
'Together round her grave we played,   55
'My brother John and I.

'And when the ground was white with snow,
'And I could run and slide,
'My brother John was forced to go,
'And he lies by her side.'   60

'How many are you then,' said I,
'If they two are in Heaven?'
The little Maiden did reply,
'O Master! we are seven.'

'But they are dead; those two are dead!   65
'Their spirits are in heaven!'
'Twas throwing words away; for still
The little Maid would have her will,
And said, 'Nay, we are seven!'

1798   1798

[1] A cloth used as a head-scarf or shawl. Originally short for 'coverchief'.
[2] A term, like 'Master' (l. 64) acknowledging gentility no less than seniority.
[3] A basin or bowl, as used especially for children's food.
[4] Dialect = 'from'.

Simon Lee, the Old Huntsman, With an Incident in Which He was Concerned

In the sweet shire of Cardigan,[1]
Not far from pleasant Ivor-hall,
An old man dwells, a little man,
I've heard he once was tall. .
Of years he has upon his back,   5
No doubt, a burthen weighty;
He says he is three score and ten,
But others say he's eighty.

A long blue livery-coat[2] has he,
That's fair behind, and fair before;   10
Yet, meet him where you will, you see
At once that he is poor.
Full five and twenty years he lived
A running huntsman merry;
And, though he has but one eye left,   15
His cheek is like a cherry.

No man like him the horn could sound,
And no man was so full of glee;
To say the least, four counties round
Had heard of Simon Lee;   20
His master's dead, and no one now
Dwells in the hall of Ivor;
Men, dogs, and horses, all are dead;
He is the sole survivor.

His hunting feats have him bereft   25
Of his right eye, as you may see:
And then, what limbs those feats have left
To poor old Simon Lee!

[1] A county in Wales. Since Wordsworth had identified Simon as 'huntsman to the Squires of Alfoxden', clearly the setting is fictionalized. 'Ivor Hall' is an imaginary stately home.
[2] Coat belonging to a uniform worn by a gentleman's servants.

He has no son, he has no child,
His wife, an aged woman,   30
Lives with him, near the waterfall,
Upon the village common.

And he is lean and he is sick,
His little body's half awry,
His ancles they are swoln and thick;   35
His legs are thin and dry.
When he was young he little knew
Of husbandry or tillage;
And now he's forced to work, though weak,
—The weakest in the village.   40

He all the country could outrun,
Could leave both man and horse behind;
And often, ere the race was done,
He reeled and was stone-blind.[1]
And still there's something in the world   45
At which his heart rejoices;
For when the chiming hounds are out,
He dearly loves their voices!

Old Ruth works out of doors with him,
And does what Simon cannot do;   50
For she, not over stout of limb,
Is stouter of the two.
And though you with your utmost skill
From labour could not wean them,
Alas! 'tis very little, all   55
Which they can do between them.

Beside their moss-grown hut of clay,
Not twenty paces from the door,
A scrap of land they have, but they
Are poorest of the poor.   60
This scrap of land he from the heath

[1] Completely blind.

Enclosed[1] when he was stronger;
But what avails the land to them,
Which they can till no longer?

Few months of life has he in store,   65
As he to you will tell,
For still, the more he works, the more
His poor old ancles swell.
My gentle[2] reader, I perceive
How patiently you've waited,   70
And I'm afraid that you expect
Some tale will be related.

O reader! had you in your mind
Such stores as silent thought can bring,
O gentle reader! you would find   75
A tale in every thing.
What more I have to say is short,
I hope you'll kindly take it;
It is no tale; but should you think,
Perhaps a tale you'll make it.   80

One summer-day I chanced to see
This old man doing all he could
About the root of an old tree,
A stump of rotten wood.
The mattock[3] totter'd in his hand;   85
So vain was his endeavour
That at the root of the old tree
He might have worked for ever.

'You're overtasked, good Simon Lee,
Give me your tool' to him I said;   90
And at the word right gladly he

---

[1] The fencing-off or enclosure of common land was a fiercely controversial subject from the mid-18th to the early 19th century.
[2] 'Gentle-hearted' or 'of noble birth'. Most of Wordsworth's readers would have been relatively well-off. The poem encourages us to reflect on the relation between gentility and gentleness.
[3] A short-handled pick-like tool, used for grubbing up trees. etc.

Received my proffer'd aid.
I struck, and with a single blow
The tangled root I sever'd,
At which the poor old man so long 95
And vainly had endeavour'd.

The tears into his eyes were brought,
And thanks and praises seemed to run
So fast out of his heart, I thought
They never would have done. 100
—I've heard of hearts unkind, kind deeds
With coldness still returning.[1]
Alas! the gratitude of men
Has oftner left me mourning.

1798   1798

The Thorn[2]

1

There is a thorn; it looks so old,
In truth you'd find it hard to say,
How it could ever have been young,
It looks so old and grey.
Not higher than a two-years' child, 5
It stands erect this aged thorn;
No leaves it has, no thorny points;
It is a mass of knotted joints,
A wretched thing forlorn.

[1] Probably a perfect rhyme with 'mourning' in Wordsworth's strong Cumbrian accent.

[2] Wordsworth maintained that the poem 'is not supposed to be spoken in the author's own person: '. . . the character of the loquacious narrator will sufficiently show itself in the course of the story' (Advertisement to *Lyrical Ballads* [1798]).

It stands erect, and like a stone
With lichens¹ it is overgrown.

2

Like rock or stone, it is o'ergrown
With lichens to the very top,
And hung with heavy tufts of moss,
A melancholy crop: 15
Up from the earth these mosses creep,
And this poor thorn they clasp it round
So close, you'd say that they were bent
With plain and manifest intent,
To drag it to the ground;   20
And all had joined in one endeavour
To bury this poor thorn for ever.

3

High on a mountain's highest ridge,
Where oft the stormy winter gale
Cuts like a scythe, while through the clouds   25
It sweeps from vale to vale;
Not five yards from the mountain-path,
This thorn you on your left espy;
And to the left, three yards beyond,
You see a little muddy pond   30
Of water, never dry;
I've measured it from side to side:
'Tis three feet long, and two feet wide.²

4

And close beside this aged thorn,
There is a fresh and lovely sight,   35
A beauteous heap, a hill of moss,
Just half a foot in height.
All lovely colours there you see,
All colours that were ever seen,
And mossy network too is there,   40

¹ Tight-knit, spreading, many-coloured mossy plants, often found on trees and stones.
² The closing two lines of this stanza have been abundantly mocked. Wordsworth in 1815 maintained that they 'ought to be liked'.

As if by hand of lady fair
The work had woven been,
And cups, the darlings of the eye,
So deep is their vermilion dye.

5

Ah me! what lovely tints are there!   45
Of olive-green and scarlet bright,
In spikes, in branches, and in stars,
Green, red, and pearly white.
This heap of earth o'ergrown with moss,
Which close beside the thorn you see,   50
So fresh in all its beauteous dyes,
Is like an infant's grave in size
As like as like can be:
But never, never any where,
An infant's grave was half so fair.   55

6

Now would you see this aged thorn,
This pond and beauteous hill of moss,
You must take care and chuse your time
The mountain when to cross.
For oft there sits, between the heap   60
That's like an infant's grave in size,
And that same pond of which I spoke,
A woman in a scarlet cloak,
And to herself she cries,
'Oh misery! oh misery!   65
'Oh woe is me! oh misery!'

7

At all times of the day and night
This wretched woman thither goes,
And she is known to every star,
And every wind that blows;   70
And there beside the thorn she sits
When the blue day-light's in the skies,
And when the whirlwind's on the hill,
Or frosty air is keen and still,

And to herself she cries,   75
'Oh misery! oh misery!
'Oh woe is me! oh misery!'

8

'Now wherefore thus, by day and night,
'In rain, in tempest, and in snow,
'Thus to the dreary mountain-top   80
'Does this poor woman go?
'And why sits she beside the thorn
'When the blue day-light's in the sky,
'Or when the whirlwind's on the hill,
'Or frosty air is keen and still,   85
'And wherefore does she cry?—
'Oh wherefore? wherefore? tell me why
'Does she repeat that doleful cry?'

9

I cannot tell; I wish I could;
For the true reason no one knows,   90
But if you'd gladly view the spot,
The spot to which she goes;
The heap that's like an infant's grave,
The pond—and thorn, so old and grey,
Pass by her door—'tis seldom shut—   95
And if you see her in her hut,
Then to the spot away!—
I never heard of such as dare
Approach the spot when she is there.

10

'But wherefore to the mountain-top   100
'Can this unhappy woman go,
'Whatever star is in the skies,
'Whatever wind may blow?'
Nay rack your brain—'tis all in vain,
I'll tell you every thing I know;   105
But to the thorn, and to the pond
Which is a little step beyond,
I wish that you would go:

Perhaps when you are at the place
You something of her tale may trace.   110

11

I'll give you the best help I can:
Before you up the mountain go,
Up to the dreary mountain-top,
I'll tell you all I know.
'Tis now some two and twenty years,   115
Since she (her name is Martha Ray)[1]
Gave with a maiden's true good will
Her company to Stephen Hill;
And she was blithe and gay,
And she was happy, happy still   120
Whene'er she thought of Stephen Hill.

12

And they had fix'd the wedding-day,
The morning that must wed them both;
But Stephen to another maid
Had sworn another oath;   125
And with this other maid to church
Unthinking Stephen went—
Poor Martha! on that woful day
A cruel, cruel fire, they say,
Into her bones was sent: 130
It dried her body like a cinder,
And almost turn'd her brain to tinder.[2]

13

They say, full six months after this,
While yet the summer-leaves were green,
She to the mountain-top would go,   135
And there was often seen.
'Tis said, a child was in her womb,
As now to any eye was plain;

[1] Also the name of the mother of Wordsworth's friend, Basil Montagu.
Widely known as the mistress of the Earl of Sandwich, she was publicly shot
by a rejected suitor in 1779.
[2] Any light, dry material, used for starting a fire.

She was with child, and she was mad,
Yet often she was sober sad   140
From her exceeding pain.
Oh me! ten thousand times I'd rather
That he had died, that cruel father!

14

Sad case for such a brain to hold
Communion with a stirring child!   145
Sad case, as you may think, for one
Who had a brain so wild!
Last Christmas when we talked of this,
Old Farmer Simpson did maintain,
That in her womb the infant wrought   150
About its mother's heart, and brought
Her senses back again:
And when at last her time drew near,
Her looks were calm, her senses clear.

15

No more I know, I wish I did,   155
And I would tell it all to you;
For what became of this poor child
There's none that ever knew:
And if a child was born or no,
There's no one that could ever tell;   160
And if 'twas born alive or dead,
There's no one knows, as I have said,
But some remember well,
That Martha Ray about this time
Would up the mountain often climb.   165

16

And all that winter, when at night
The wind blew from the mountain-peak,
'Twas worth your while, though in the dark,
The church-yard path to seek:
For many a time and oft were heard   170
Cries coming from the mountain-head,
Some plainly living voices were,

And others, I've heard many swear,
Were voices of the dead:
I cannot think, whate'er they say,   175
They had to do with Martha Ray.

17

But that she goes to this old thorn,
The thorn which I've described to you,
And there sits in a scarlet cloak,
I will be sworn is true.   180
For one day with my telescope,
To view the ocean wide and bright,
When to this country first I came,
Ere I had heard of Martha's name,
I climbed the mountain's height: 185
A storm came on, and I could see
No object higher than my knee.

18

'Twas mist and rain, and storm and rain,
No screen, no fence could I discover,
And then the wind! in faith, it was   190
A wind full ten times over.
I looked around, I thought I saw
A jutting crag, and off I ran,
Head-foremost, through the driving rain,
The shelter of the crag to gain,   195
And, as I am a man,
Instead of jutting crag, I found
A woman seated on the ground.

19

I did not speak—I saw her face,
Her face it was enough for me;   200
I turned about and heard her cry,
'O misery! O misery!'
And there she sits, until the moon
Through half the clear blue sky will go,
And when the little breezes make   205
The waters of the pond to shake,

As all the country know,
She shudders and you hear her cry,
'Oh misery! oh misery!'

20

'But what's the thorn? and what's the pond?   210
'And what's the hill of moss to her?
'And what's the creeping breeze that comes
'The little pond to stir?'
I cannot tell; but some will say
She hanged her baby on the tree,   215
Some say she drowned it in the pond,
Which is a little step beyond,
But all and each agree,
The little babe was buried there,
Beneath that hill of moss so fair.   220

21

I've heard the scarlet moss is red
With drops of that poor infant's blood;
But kill a new-born infant thus!
I do not think she could.
Some say, if to the pond you go,   225
And fix on it a steady view,
The shadow of a babe you trace,
A baby and a baby's face,
And that it looks at you;
Whene'er you look on it, 'tis plain   230
The baby looks at you again.

22

And some had sworn an oath that she
Should be to public justice brought;
And for the little infant's bones
With spades they would have sought.   235
But then the beauteous hill of moss
Before their eyes began to stir;
And for full fifty yards around,
The grass it shook upon the ground;
But all do still aver   240

The little babe is buried there,
Beneath that hill of moss so fair.

                    23
I cannot tell how this may be,
But plain it is, the thorn is bound
With heavy tufts of moss, that strive   245
To drag it to the ground.
And this I know, full many a time,
When she was on the mountain high,
By day, and in the silent night,
When all the stars shone clear and bright,   250
That I have heard her cry,
'Oh misery! oh misery!
'Oh woe is me! oh misery!'

  1798   1798

Lines Written In Early Spring

I heard a thousand blended notes,[1]
While in a grove I sate reclined,
In that sweet mood when pleasant thoughts
Bring sad thoughts to the mind.

To her fair works did nature link   5
The human soul that through me ran;
And much it griev'd my heart to think
What man has made of man.

Through primrose-tufts, in that sweet bower,
The periwinkle trail'd its wreathes;   10
And 'tis my faith that every flower
Enjoys the air it breathes.

[1] Wordsworth in a letter once spelled 'note' 'naught' indicating a
pronunciation that would have rhymed exactly with 'thought'.

The birds around me hopp'd and play'd:
Their thoughts I cannot measure,
But the least motion which they made,   15
It seem'd a thrill of pleasure.

The budding twigs spread out their fan,
To catch the breezy air;
And I must think, do all I can,
That there was pleasure there.   20

If I these thoughts may not prevent,
If such be of my creed[1] the plan,[2]
Have I not reason to lament
What man has made of man?

1798   1798

Expostulation and Reply

'Why William,[3] on that old grey stone,
'Thus for the length of half a day,
'Why William, sit you thus alone,
'And dream your time away?

'Where are your books? that light[4] bequeath'd   5
'To beings else forlorn and blind!
'Up! Up! and drink the spirit breath'd
'From dead men to their kind.

'You look round on your mother earth,
'As if she for no purpose bore you;   10

---

[1] 'Creed', with 'soul' (l. 6), and 'faith' (l. 11) sustains a religious undertone.
[2] Lines 21–2 were changed in 1820 to 'If this belief from Heaven is sent, / If such be nature's holy plan.'.
[3] Wordsworth presents himself as being expostulated *with* by 'Matthew'.
[4] Cp. 'Elegiac Stanzas', ll. 15–16.

'As if you were her first-born birth,
'And none had lived before you!'

One morning thus, by Esthwaite lake,
When life was sweet I knew not why,
To me my good friend Matthew spake,[1]   15
And thus I made reply.

'The eye it cannot chuse but see,
'We cannot bid the ear be still;
'Our bodies feel, where'er they be,
'Against, or with our will.   20

'Nor less I deem that there are powers,
'Which of themselves our minds impress,[2]
'That we can feed this mind of ours,
'In a wise passiveness.

'Think you, mid all this mighty sum   25
'Of things for ever speaking,
'That nothing of itself will come,
'But we must still be seeking?

'—Then ask not wherefore, here, alone,
'Conversing as I may,   30
'I sit upon this old grey stone,
'And dream my time away.'

1798   1798

[1] In 1798 Wordsworth said the poem 'arose out of conversation with a
friend who was somewhat unreasonably attached to modern books of Moral
Philosophy.'
[2] Wordsworth conceived of the mind as equally able to make physical
impressions on the world and to receive physical impressions from it. Cp.
'Tintern Abbey'. ll. 5–7: '... cliffs / Which on a wild secluded scene impress /
Thoughts ...'.

The Tables Turned

An Evening Scene, on the Same Subject[1]

Up! up! my friend, and clear your looks,
Why all this toil and trouble?
Up! up! my friend, and quit your books,
Or surely you'll grow double.

The sun above the mountain's head,   5
A freshening lustre mellow,
Through all the long green fields has spread,
His first sweet evening yellow.

Books! 'tis a dull and endless strife,
Come, hear the woodland linnet,   10
How sweet his music; on my life
There's more of wisdom in it.

And hark! how blithe the throstle[2] sings!
And he is no mean preacher;
Come forth into the light of things,   15
Let Nature[3] be your teacher.

She has a world of ready wealth,
Our minds and hearts to bless—
Spontaneous wisdom breathed by health,
Truth breathed by chearfulness.   20

One impulse from a vernal wood
May teach you more of man:
Of moral evil and of good,
Than all the sages can.

[1] A companion-piece to 'Expostulation and Reply': Wordsworth admonishes Matthew.
[2] The thrush, especially the song-thrush.
[3] Here there is a potential for creative ambiguity between two main senses of 'nature': human nature and 'material' nature, or landscape.

Sweet is the lore which nature brings;   25
Our meddling intellect[1]
Mishapes the beauteous forms of things;
—We murder to dissect.

Enough of science[2] and of art;
Close up these barren leaves;[3]   30
Come forth, and bring with you a heart
That watches and receives.

1798   1798

Lines Written a Few Miles Above Tintern Abbey, on Revisiting the Banks of the Wye During a Tour, July 13, 1798

Five years have passed; five summers, with the length
Of five long winters! and again I hear
These waters rolling from their mountain-springs
With a sweet inland murmur.[4]—Once again
Do I behold these steep and lofty cliffs,   5
Which on a wild secluded scene impress
Thoughts of more deep seclusion; and connect
The landscape with the quiet of the sky.
The day is come when I again repose
Here, under this dark sycamore, and view   10
These plots of cottage-ground, these orchard-tufts,
Which, at this season, with their unripe fruits,
Among the woods and copses lose themselves,
Nor, with their green and simple hue, disturb

[1] 'Intellect', unlike 'reason', is often derogatory in Wordsworth's writing.
[2] Learning in general (from Latin *scire* to know).
[3] With a punning hint that tree-leaves, unlike book-leaves, *aren't* 'barren'.
[4] 'The river is not affected by the tides a few miles above Tintern'
(Wordsworth's note).

The wild green landscape. Once again I see   15
These hedge-rows, hardly hedge-rows, little lines
Of sportive wood run wild; these pastoral farms
Green to the very door; and wreathes of smoke
Sent up, in silence, from among the trees,
With some uncertain notice, as might seem   20
Of vagrant dwellers in the houseless woods,
Or of some hermit's cave, where by his fire
The hermit sits alone.
                         Though absent long,
These forms of beauty have not been to me,
As is a landscape to a blind man's eye: 25
But oft, in lonely rooms, and mid the din
Of towns and cities, I have owed to them,
In hours of weariness, sensations sweet,
Felt in the blood, and felt along[1] the heart,
And passing even into my purer mind   30
With tranquil restoration:—feelings too
Of unremembered pleasure; such, perhaps,
As may have had no trivial influence
On that best portion of a good man's life;
His little, nameless, unremembered acts   35
Of kindness and of love. Nor less, I trust,
To them I may have owed another gift,
Of aspect more sublime; that blessed mood,
In which the burthen of the mystery,
In which the heavy and the weary weight   40
Of all this unintelligible world
Is lighten'd:—that serene and blessed mood,
In which the affections gently lead us on,
Until, the breath of this corporeal[2] frame,
And even the motion of our human blood   45
Almost suspended, we are laid asleep
In body, and become a living soul:
While with an eye made quiet by the power
Of harmony, and the deep power of joy,
We see into the life of things.   50
                         If this

[1] 'Along' ascribes length to the 'heart', thereby prolonging its sensations.
[2] 'physical' (from Latin corpus, body): stressed on the second syllable.

Be but a vain belief, yet, oh! how oft,
In darkness, and amid the many shapes
Of joyless day-light; when the fretful stir
Unprofitable, and the fever of the world,
Have hung upon the beatings of my heart,   55
How oft, in spirit, have I turned to thee
O sylvan[1] Wye! Thou wanderer through the woods,
How often has my spirit turned to thee!

And now, with gleams of half-extinguish'd thought,
With many recognitions dim and faint,   60
And somewhat of a sad perplexity,
The picture of the mind revives again:
While here I stand, not only with the sense
Of present pleasure, but with pleasing thoughts
That in this moment there is life and food   65
For future years. And so I dare to hope
Though changed, no doubt, from what I was, when first
I came among these hills; when like a roe
I bounded o'er the mountains, by the sides
Of the deep rivers, and the lonely streams,   70
Wherever nature led; more like a man
Flying from something that he dreads, than one
Who sought the thing he loved. For nature then
(The coarser pleasures of my boyish days,
And their glad animal[2] movements all gone by,)   75
To me was all in all.—I cannot paint
What then I was. The sounding cataract
Haunted me like a passion: the tall rock,
The mountain, and the deep and gloomy wood,
Their colours and their forms, were then to me   80
An appetite: a feeling and a love,
That had no need of a remoter charm,

[1] Literally 'woodland-inhabiting': but because of its archaic use as a noun meaning 'mythological being frequenting woods', and its association by sound with 'sylph' and 'silver'. 'sylvan' has connotations of mystery. delicacy and beauty.
[2] See headnote to 'Old Man Travelling'. Clearly used here to mean 'bodily'. with a hint of 'animal-like'.

By thought supplied, or any interest
Unborrowed from the eye.—That time is past,
And all its aching joys are now no more,   85
And all its dizzy raptures. Not for this
Faint I, nor mourn nor murmur: other gifts
Have followed, for such loss, I would believe,
Abundant recompence. For I have learned
To look on nature, not as in the hour   90
Of thoughtless youth, but hearing oftentimes
The still, sad music of humanity,
Not harsh nor grating, though of ample power
To chasten and subdue. And I have felt
A presence that disturbs me with the joy   95
Of elevated thoughts; a sense sublime
Of something far more deeply interfused,
Whose dwelling is the light of setting suns,
And the round ocean, and the living air,
And the blue sky, and in[1] the mind of man,   100
A motion and a spirit, that impels
All thinking things, all objects of all thought,
And rolls through all things. Therefore am I still
A lover of the meadows and the woods,
And mountains; and of all that we behold   105
From this green earth; of all the mighty world
Of eye and ear, both what they half-create,
And what perceive; well pleased to recognize
In nature and the language of the sense,[2]
The anchor of my purest thoughts, the nurse,   110
The guide, the guardian of my heart, and soul
Of all my moral being.

                    Nor, perchance,
If I were not thus taught, should I the more
Suffer my genial[3] spirits to decay: 115

---

[1] The 'in' subtly differentiates 'the mind' from the external dwelling-places.
[2] 'Senses', but also 'moral sense' or intuition.
[3] Cp. Milton, *Samson Agonistes*, l. 594: 'So much I feel my genial spirits
droop'. The word spans its older senses of a) 'pertaining to "genius" or
temperament', b) 'creative' and its still-current sense of c) 'good-humoured'.

For thou art with me,[1] here, upon the banks
Of this fair river; thou, my dearest Friend,
My dear, dear Friend, and in thy voice I catch
The language of my former heart, and read
My former pleasures in the shooting lights   120
Of thy wild eyes. Oh! yet a little while
May I behold in thee what I was once,
My dear, dear Sister! And this prayer I make,
Knowing that Nature never did betray
The heart that loved her; 'tis her privilege,   125
Through all the years of this our life, to lead
From joy to joy: for she can so inform
The mind that is within us, so impress
With quietness and beauty, and so feed
With lofty thoughts, that neither evil tongues,[2]   130
Rash judgments, nor the sneers of selfish men,
Nor greetings where no kindness is, nor all
The dreary intercourse of daily life,
Shall e'er prevail against us, or disturb
Our chearful faith that all which we behold   135
Is full of blessings. Therefore let the moon
Shine on thee in thy solitary walk;
And let the misty mountain winds be free
To blow against thee: and in after years,
When these wild ecstasies shall be matured   140
Into a sober pleasure, when thy mind
Shall be a mansion[3] for all lovely forms,
Thy memory be as a dwelling-place
For all sweet sounds and harmonies; Oh! then,
If solitude, or fear, or pain, or grief,   145
Should be thy portion, with what healing thoughts
Of tender joy wilt thou remember me,
And these my exhortations! Nor, perchance,
If I should be, where I no more can hear

[1] Cp. *Psalms* 23:4: 'for thou art with me; thy rod and thy staff they
comfort me.' The rest of the poem is explicitly addressed to Dorothy
Wordsworth.
[2] Cp. Milton. *Paradise Lost.* vii. 26: 'On evil days though fallen. and evil
tongues'.
[3] An abiding-place.

Thy voice, nor catch from thy wild eyes these gleams   150
Of past existence, wilt thou then forget
That on the banks of this delightful stream
We stood together; and that I, so long
A worshipper of Nature, hither came,
Unwearied in that service: rather say   155
With warmer love, oh! with far deeper zeal
Of holier love. Nor wilt thou then forget,
That after many wanderings, many years
Of absence, these steep woods and lofty cliffs,
And this green pastoral landscape, were to me   160
More dear, both for themselves, and for thy sake.

1798   1798

[A slumber did my spirit seal][1]

A slumber did my spirit seal
  I had no human fears:
She seem'd a thing that could not feel
  The touch of earthly years.

No motion has she now, no force;   5
  She neither hears nor sees;
Roll'd round in earth's diurnal[2] course,
  With rocks, and stones and trees!

1798   1800

[1] One of five 'Lucy' poems. Coleridge wrote to a friend (6 April 1799):
'Some months ago Wordsworth transmitted to me a most sublime epitaph—
whether it had any reality. I cannot say.—Most probably, in some gloomier
moment he had fancied the moment in which his sister might die.'
[2] 'Occurring daily', with perhaps a grief-stricken glance at the word 'urn'.

Song[1]

She dwelt among th' untrodden ways
   Beside the springs of Dove,[2]
A Maid whom there were none to praise
   And very few to love.

A Violet by a mossy Stone   5
   Half-hidden from the Eye!
—Fair as a star when only one
   Is shining in the sky!

She *liv'd* unknown, and few could know
   When Lucy ceas'd to be;   10
But she is in her Grave, and, oh!
   The difference to me.

1798   1800

[Strange fits of passion I have known][3]

   Strange fits of passion I have known,
   And I will dare to tell,
   But in the lover's ear alone,
   What once to me befel.

   When she I lov'd, was strong and gay   5
   And like a rose in June,
   I to her cottage bent my way,
   Beneath the evening moon.

[1] An earlier draft contains two extra stanzas, the first of which originally opened the poem: 'My hope was one, from cities far, / Nursed on a lonesome heath: / Her lips are red as roses are, / Her hair a woodbine wreath.'

[2] There are three rivers in England with this name.

[3] The manuscript title 'A Reverie' was deleted before publication.

Upon the moon I fix'd my eye,
All over the wide lea;[1]   10
My horse trudg'd on, and we drew nigh
Those paths so dear to me.

And now we reach'd the orchard-plot,
And, as we climb'd the hill,
Towards the roof of Lucy's cot[2]   15
The moon descended still.

In one of those sweet dreams I slept,
Kind Nature's gentlest boon!
And, all the while, my eyes I kept
On the descending moon.   20

My horse mov'd on; hoof after hoof
He rais'd, and never stopp'd:
When down behind the cottage roof
At once, the planet dropped.

What fond and wayward thoughts will slide   25
Into a Lover's head –
'O mercy!' to myself I cried,
'If Lucy should be dead!'[3]

1798   1800

[1] Meadow: pasture or uncultivated grassland.
[2] 'cottage'. but with a suggestion, perhaps, of 'bed'.
[3] A draft ends with the stanza: 'I told her this: her laughter light / Is ringing in my ears; / And when I think upon that night / My eyes are dim with tears.'

Nutting[1]

———————————It seems a day,
One of those heavenly days that cannot die,
When forth I sallied from our cottage-door,[2]
And with a wallet[3] o'er my shoulder slung,
A nutting crook[4] in hand, I turn'd my steps   5
Towards the distant woods, a Figure quaint,
Trick'd out in proud disguise of Beggar's weeds[5]
Put on for the occasion, by advice
And exhortation of my frugal Dame.[6]
Motley accoutrement![7] of power to smile   10
At thorns, and brakes,[8] and brambles, and, in truth,
More ragged than need was. Among the woods,
And o'er the pathless rocks, I forc'd my way
Until, at length, I came to one dear nook
Unvisited, where not a broken bough   15
Droop'd with its wither'd leaves, ungracious sign
Of devastation; but the hazels rose
Tall and erect, with milk-white clusters hung,
A virgin scene!—A little while I stood,
Breathing with such suppression of the heart   20
As joy delights in; and with wise restraint
Voluptuous, fearless of a rival, eyed
The banquet, or beneath the trees I sate

[1] '. . . intended as part of a poem on my own life [probably *The Prelude*], but struck out as not being wanted there.' (Wordsworth, 1843). Wordsworth considered that this poem and 'To Joanna' 'show the greatest genius of any poems in the second volume' of *Lyrical Ballads* (1800).

[2] 'The house at which I was boarded during the time I was at School' Wordsworth's note (1800) thus unequivocally identifies him with the 'I' of the poem.

[3] Bag.

[4] A hooked stick for use in gathering nuts.

[5] Clothes: an archaism Wordsworth would probably have associated with Chaucer.

[6] Wordsworth is almost certainly thinking of Ann Tyson, with whom he lodged while at school in Hawkshead. See his tribute to her in *The Prelude* (1805). iv. 207–21.

[7] Unsightly (because ill-matching) outfit.

[8] Patches of rough, overgrown land.

Among the flowers, and with the flowers I play'd;
A temper[1] known to those, who, after long   25
And weary expectation, have been bless'd
With sudden happiness beyond all hope.—
—Perhaps it was a bower beneath whose leaves
The violets of five seasons reappear
And fade, unseen by any human eye,   30
Where fairy water-breaks[2] do murmur on
For ever, and I saw the sparkling foam,
And with my cheek on one of those green stones
That, fleec'd with moss, beneath the shady trees
Lay round me scatter'd like a flock of sheep,   35
I heard the murmur and the murmuring sound,
In that sweet mood when pleasure loves to pay
Tribute to ease, and, of its joy secure,
The heart luxuriates with indifferent things,
Wasting its kindliness on stocks and stones,   40
And on the vacant air.—Then up I rose,
And dragg'd to earth both branch and bough, with crash
And merciless ravage,[3] and the shady nook
Of hazels, and the green and mossy bower,
Deform'd and sullied, patiently gave up   45
Their quiet being: and unless I now
Confound my present feelings with the past,
Even then, when from the bower I turn'd away,
Exulting, rich beyond the wealth of kings—
I felt a sense of pain when I beheld   50
The silent trees and the intruding sky.—

Then, dearest Maiden,[4] move along these shades
In gentleness of heart; with gentle hand
Touch,—for there is a Spirit in the woods.

1798   1800

[1] Mood. (Cp. 'temperament').
[2] Stretches of broken water. This sense coined by Wordsworth, the example
here pre-dating the one from 1806 in OED.
[3] The sexual connotations of this word bring to the surface an
undercurrent of sexual innuendo discernible from at least l. 20 onwards.
[4] The 'dearest maiden' (l. 52) is named 'Lucy' in discarded manuscript
lines.

Ruth

When Ruth was left half desolate,
Her Father took another Mate;
And so, not seven years old,
The slighted Child, at her own will
Went wandering over dale and hill,   5
In thoughtless freedom bold.

And she had made a pipe of straw
And from that oaten pipe[1] could draw
All sounds of winds and floods;
Had built a bower upon the green,   10
As if she from her birth had been
An Infant of the woods.

There came a Youth[2] from Georgia's shore –
A military casque[3] he wore,
With splendid feathers drest;   15
He brought them from the Cherokees;
The feathers nodded in the breeze
And made a gallant crest.

From Indian blood you deem him sprung.
Ah no! he spake the English tongue   20
And bare a Soldier's name;
And when America was free
From battle and from jeopardy,
He cross the ocean came.

With hues of genius on his cheek   25
In finest tones the Youth could speak.—
—While he was yet a Boy
The moon, the glory of the sun,

[1] Flutes made out of hollow oat-stems are common in pastoral poetry.
[2] He is never named.
[3] Helmet.

And streams that murmur as they run,
Had been his dearest joy.   30

He was a lovely Youth! I guess
The panther in the wilderness[1]
Was not so fair as he;
And when he chose to sport and play,
No dolphin ever was so gay   35
Upon the tropic sea.

Among the Indians he had fought,
And with him many tales he brought
Of pleasure and of fear,
Such tales as told to any Maid   40
By such a Youth in the green shade[2]
Were perilous to hear.

He told of Girls, a happy rout,[3]
Who quit their fold with dance and shout,
Their pleasant Indian town,   45
To gather strawberries all day long,
Returning with a choral song
When day-light is gone down.

He spake of plants divine and strange
That every day their blossoms change,   50
Ten thousand lovely hues!
With budding, fading, faded flowers
They stand the wonder of the bowers
From morn to evening dews.

He told of the magnolia,[4] spread   55
High as a cloud, high over head!
The cypress and her spire,

[1] The predatory comparison is ominous.
[2] Cp. Andrew Marvell. 'The Garden'. ll. 47–8: 'Annihilating all that's made
/ For a green thought in a green shade.' The echo suggests a paradisal setting.
[3] Noisy crowd.
[4] 'Magnolia grandiflora' (Wordsworth). None of the many species of
magnolia is now native in Europe. This one is described in William Bartram.
Travels Through North and South Carolina. Georgia. etc. (1791) – see note p. 41.

Of flowers that with one scarlet gleam[1]
Cover a hundred leagues and seem
To set the hills on fire.   60

The Youth of green Savannahs spake,
And many an endless endless lake,
With all its fairy crowds
Of islands that together lie
As quietly as spots of sky   65
Among the evening clouds.

And then he said, 'How sweet it were
A fisher or a hunter there,
A gardener in the shade,
Still wandering with an easy mind   70
To build a household fire and find
A home in every glade.

What days and what sweet years! Ah me
Our life were life indeed, with thee
So pass'd in quiet bliss,   75
And all the while' said he 'to know
That we were in a world of woe,[2]
On such an earth as this!'

And then he sometimes interwove
Dear thoughts about a father's love: 80
'For there,' said he, 'are spun
Around the heart such tender ties
That our own children to our eyes
Are dearer than the sun.

Sweet Ruth! and could you go with me   85
My helpmate in the woods to be,
Our shed at night to rear;

[1] Azaleas. 'The splendid appearance of these scarlet flowers, which are scattered with such profusion over the hills in the southern part of North America, is frequently mentioned by Bartram in his Travels' (Wordsworth).

[2] Cp. *Paradise Lost*, ix. 11: on the events 'That brought into this world a world of woe'. Another glance at a paradise about to be lost.

Or run, my own adopted bride,
A sylvan huntress at my side
And drive the flying deer!   90

Beloved Ruth!' No more he said.
Sweet Ruth alone at midnight shed
A solitary tear,
She thought again—and did agree
With him to sail across the sea,   95
And drive the flying deer.

'And now, as fitting is and right,
We in the Church our faith will plight,[1]
A Husband and a Wife.'
Even so they did; and I may say   100
That to sweet Ruth that happy day
Was more than human life.

Through dream and vision did she sink,
Delighted all the while to think
That on those lonesome floods[2]   105
And green Savannahs[3] she should share
His board[4] with lawful joy, and bear
His name in the wild woods.

But, as you have before been told,
This Stripling, sportive gay and bold,   110
And, with his dancing crest,
So beautiful, through savage lands
Had roam'd about with vagrant bands
Of Indians in the West.

The wind, the tempest roaring high,   115
The tumult of a tropic sky
Might well be dangerous food
For him, a Youth to whom was given

[1] Promise fidelity to each other and to God.
[2] Big rivers.
[3] Vast treeless grasslands in the tropical parts of north and south America.
[4] Table: hence food, as in 'board and lodging'.

So much of earth so much of heaven,
And such impetuous blood.   120

Whatever in those climes he found
Irregular in sight or sound
Did to his mind impart
A kindred impulse,[1] seem'd allied
To his own powers, and justified   125
The workings of his heart.

Nor less, to feed voluptuous thought[2]
The beauteous forms of Nature wrought,
Fair trees and lovely flowers;
The breezes their own languor lent;   130
The stars had feelings, which they sent
Into those magic bowers.

Yet, in his worst pursuits, I ween[3]
That sometimes there did intervene
Pure hopes of high intent: 135
For passions link'd to forms so fair
And stately, needs must have their share
Of noble sentiment.

But ill he lived, much evil saw
With men to whom no better law[4]   140
Nor better life was known;
Deliberately, and undeceiv'd
Those wild men's vices he receiv'd,
And gave them back his own.

His genius[5] and his moral frame[6]   145
Were thus impair'd, and he became

[1] See 'A Poet's Epitaph'. l. 47 and note.
[2] Thought leading from sensuous to sensual pleasures.
[3] 'Believe': archaic usage. probably associated by Wordsworth with Chaucer.
[4] Cp. 'The Old Cumberland Beggar'. l. 128 and note. Wordsworth often
uses the word 'law' in a sense deriving from St Paul: 'the [moral] law written
in [our] hearts.' (*Romans* 2:15).
[5] The spirit informing his temperament.
[6] State. disposition.

The slave of low desires;
A man who without self-controul
Would seek what the degraded soul
Unworthily admires.   150

And yet he with no feign'd delight
Had woo'd the Maiden, day and night
Had loved her, night and morn;
What could he less than love a Maid
Whose heart with so much nature[1] play'd   155
So kind and so forlorn?

But now the pleasant dream was gone,
No hope, no wish remain'd, not one,
They stirr'd him now no more,
New objects did new pleasure give,   160
And once again he wish'd to live
As lawless as before.

Meanwhile, as thus with him it fared
They for the voyage were prepared
And went to the sea-shore,   165
But, when they thither came, the Youth
Deserted his poor Bride, and Ruth[2]
Could never find him more.

'God help thee, Ruth!'[3]—Such pains she had
That she in half a year was mad   170
And in a prison hous'd;
And there, exulting in her wrongs,
Among the music of her songs
She fearfully carouz'd.

Yet sometimes milder hours she knew,   175
Nor wanted sun, nor rain, nor dew,
Nor pastimes of the May,

[1] a) good nature; b) naturalness; and, perhaps faintly, c) beautiful scenery.
[2] The only time the couple rhyme. Ruth is now, like her biblical namesake, exiled.
[3] The inverted commas suggest an impassioned outburst from the narrator.

They all were with her in her cell,
And a wild brook with chearful knell
Did o'er the pebbles play.   180

When Ruth three seasons thus had lain
There came a respite to her pain,
She from her prison fled;
But of the Vagrant none took thought,
And where it liked her best she sought   185
Her shelter and her bread.

Among the fields she breathed again:
The master-current of her brain
Ran permanent and free,
And, coming to the Banks of Tone,[1]   190
She took her way, to dwell alone
Under the greenwood tree.[2]

The engines[3] of her grief, the tools
That shap'd her sorrow, rocks and pools,
And airs that gently stir   195
The vernal leaves, she loved them still,
Nor ever taxed them with the ill
Which had been done to her.

A Barn her *winter* bed supplies;
But, till the warmth of summer skies   200
And summer days is gone,
(And in this tale we all agree)
She sleeps beneath the greenwood tree,
And other home hath none.

If she is press'd by want of food   205

---

[1] 'The Tone is a river of Somersetshire at no great distance from the
Quantock Hills. These hills, which are alluded to a few stanzas below, are
extremely beautiful, and in most places richly covered with coppice woods'
(Wordsworth).
[2] A stock phrase in songs and ballads (e.g. *As You Like It*, ii.5.1–8). Here, a
poignant symbol of Arcadian retreat.
[3] Products of ingenuity, contrivances, hence causes (without the current
mechanical connotations).

She from her dwelling in the wood
Repairs to a road side,
And there she begs at one steep place,
Where up and down with easy pace
The horseman-travellers ride.   210

That oaten pipe of hers is mute,
Or thrown away, but with a flute
Her loneliness she cheers;
This flute made of a hemlock[1] stalk
At evening in his homeward walk   215
The Quantock[2] Woodman hears.

I, too, have pass'd her on the hills
Setting her little water-mills
By spouts and fountains wild,
Such small machinery as she turn'd   220
Ere she had wept, ere she had mourn'd,
A young and happy Child!

Farewell! and when thy days are told[3]
Ill-fated Ruth, in hallow'd mold
Thy corpse shall buried be,   225
For thee a funeral bell shall ring,
And all the congregation sing
A Christian[4] psalm for thee. —

1798–9   1800

[1] Grimly pathetic, since all parts of the hemlock plant are highly poisonous.
[2] The Quantocks are a range of hills in Somerset.
[3] Finished; and also narrated.
[4] Affirms the religious outlook implicit in the choice of Ruth's name.

The Two April Mornings

We walk'd along, while bright and red
Uprose the morning sun,
And Mathew stopp'd, he look'd, and said,
'The will of God be done!'

A village Schoolmaster was he,[1]   5
With hair of glittering grey;
As blithe a man as you could see
On a spring holiday.

And on that morning, through the grass,
And by the steaming rills,   10
We travell'd merrily to pass
A day among the hills.

'Our work,' said I, 'was well begun;
Then, from thy breast what thought,
Beneath so beautiful a sun,   15
So sad a sigh has brought?'

A second time did Matthew stop
And fixing still his eye
Upon the eastern mountain-top
To me he made reply.   20

'Yon cloud with that long purple cleft
Brings fresh into my mind
A day like this which I have left
Full thirty years behind.

And on that slope of springing corn   25
The self-same crimson hue

---

[1] '... this Schoolmaster was made up of several both of his class and men of other occupations ... It is enough if, being true and consistent in spirit. they move and teach in a manner not unworthy of a Poet's calling.' (Wordsworth. 1843).

Fell from the sky, that April morn,
The same which now I view!

With rod and line my silent sport
I plied by Derwent's wave,[1]   30
And, coming to the church, stopp'd short
Beside my Daughter's grave.

Nine summers had she scarcely seen,
The pride of all the vale;
And then she sang!—she would have been   35
A very nightingale.—

Six feet in earth my Emma lay,[2]
And yet I lov'd her more,
For so it seem'd, than till that day
I e'er had lov'd before.   40

And, turning from her grave, I met,
Beside the church-yard Yew,
A blooming Girl, whose hair was wet
With points of morning dew.

A basket on her head she bare,   45
Her brow was smooth and white,
To see a Child so very fair,
It was a pure delight!

No fountain from its rocky cave
E'er tripp'd with foot so free,   50
She seem'd as happy as a wave
That dances on the sea.

There came from me a sigh of pain
Which I could ill confine;

---

[1] The river Derwent still runs along the back-garden of Wordsworth's childhood home in Cockermouth.

[2] The name 'Emma'. like 'Lucy' is strongly associated with Dorothy Wordsworth.

I look'd at her, and look'd again;   55
—And did not wish her mine!'[1]

Mathew is in his grave, yet now,
Methinks, I see him stand,
As at that moment, with his bough
Of wilding[2] in his hand.   60

1798   1800

A Poet's Epitaph

Art thou a Statesman[3] in the van[4]
Of public business train'd and bred,
—First learn to love one living man;
Then may'st thou think upon the dead.

A Lawyer art thou?—draw not nigh;   5
Go, carry to some other place
The hardness of thy coward eye,
The falsehood of thy sallow face.

Art thou a man of purple cheer?
A rosy man, right plump to see?   10
Approach; yet, Doctor,[5] not too near,
This grave no cushion is for thee.

Art thou a man of gallant pride,

---

[1] Matthew says the opposite of what is expected: an act of self-denial in which are implicit a faith and fortitude which the poem invites us to admire.
[2] Generally, any wild plant. More specifically, a wild apple tree, or crab-apple tree.
[3] A politician.
[4] Vanguard, or forefront.
[5] Commonly taken to mean 'Doctor of Divinity', but 'learned man' or even 'don' is possible.

A Soldier and no man of chaff?[1]
Welcome!—but lay thy sword aside,   15
And lean upon a Peasant's staff.

Physician art thou? One, all eyes,
Philosopher![2] a fingering slave,
One that would peep and botanize
Upon his mother's grave?   20

Wrapt closely in thy sensual fleece[3]
O turn aside, and take, I pray,
That he below may rest in peace,
Thy pin-point of a soul away!

—A Moralist[4] perchance appears;   25
Led, Heaven knows how! to this poor sod:[5]
And *He* has neither eyes nor ears;
Himself his world, and his own God;

One to whose smooth-rubb'd soul can cling
Nor form nor[6] feeling great nor small,   30
A reasoning, self-sufficing thing,
An intellectual All in All![7]

Shut close the door! press down the latch:
Sleep in thy intellectual crust,[8]
Nor lose ten tickings of thy watch   35
Near this unprofitable dust.

But who is He, with modest looks,

[1] Husks of wheat: the worthless part of a thing: a biblical usage.
[2] 'Natural philosopher' was the current term for physical scientist.
[3] Cosseted in fur-lined clothing, with a hint of sheep-like conventionality.
[4] Exponent of a too rigidly defined ethical system.
[5] Turf (on top of the grave): the modern slang use of 'sod' was not yet current.
[6] 'Nor ... nor' = neither ... nor.
[7] The poem deplores excessive reliance on intellect as a means of moral insight.
[8] Impenetrable outer coating.

And clad in homely russet brown?[1]
He murmurs near the running brooks
A music sweeter than their own.   40

He is retired as noontide dew,
Or fountain in a noonday grove;
And you must love him, ere to you
He will seem worthy of your love.

The outward shews of sky and earth,   45
Of hill and valley he has view'd;
And impulses of deeper birth
Have come to him in solitude.

In common things that round us lie
Some random truths he can impart,   50
The harvest of a quiet eye
That broods and sleeps on his own heart.

But he is weak, both man and boy,
Hath been an idler in the land;
Contented if he might enjoy   55
The things which others understand.

—Come hither in thy hour of strength,
Come, weak as is a breaking wave!
Here stretch thy body at full length;
Or build thy house upon this grave.—   60

1798   1800

---

[1] Clothing characteristic of the wandering bard in such poems as James
Thomson's *The Castle of Indolence* (1748) and perhaps of biblical prophets.

[Three years she grew in sun and shower]

Three years she grew in sun and shower,
Then Nature said, 'A lovelier flower
On earth was never sown:
This Child I to myself will take,
She shall be mine, and I will make   5
A Lady of my own.

Myself will to my darling be
Both law and impulse, and with me
The Girl, in rock and plain,
In earth and heaven, in glade and bower,   10
Shall feel an overseeing power
To kindle or restrain.

She shall be sportive as the fawn
That wild with glee across the lawn
Or up the mountain springs,   15
And hers shall be the breathing balm
And hers the silence and the calm
Of mute insensate[1] things.

The floating clouds their state[2] shall lend
To her, for her the willow bend,   20
Nor shall she fail to see
Even in the motions of the storm
A beauty that shall mould her form
By silent sympathy.

The stars of midnight shall be dear   25
To her, and she shall lean her ear
In many a secret place
Where rivulets dance their wayward round,
And beauty born of murmuring sound
Shall pass into her face.   30

[1] Incapable of sensation or feeling, like stones or (arguably) trees.
[2] 'Stateliness', as well as 'softness and delicacy of constitution'.

And vital feelings of delight
Shall rear her form to stately height,
Her virgin bosom swell;
Such thoughts to Lucy I will give
While she and I together live   35
Here in this happy dell.'

Thus Nature spake—The work was done—
How soon my Lucy's race was run!
She died and left to me
This heath, this calm and quiet scene,   40
The memory of what has been,
And never more will be.——

1798–9   1800

Michael, A Pastoral Poem

If from the public way you turn your steps
Up the tumultuous brook of Green-head Gill,[1]
You will suppose that with an upright path
Your feet must struggle; in such bold ascent
The pastoral Mountains front you, face to face.   5
But, courage! for beside that boisterous Brook
The Mountains have all open'd out themselves,
And made a hidden valley of their own.
No habitation there is seen; but such
As journey thither find themselves alone   10
With a few sheep, with rocks and stones, and kites[2]
That overhead are sailing in the Sky.
It is in truth an utter solitude.
Nor should I have made mention of this Dell
But for one object which you might pass by,   15

[1] A gill or ghyll (Wordsworth's usual spelling) is a narrow mountain
torrent.
[2] The hawk-like birds of prey, not the air-borne toys on a string.

Might see and notice not. Beside the brook
There is a straggling Heap of unhewn stones;
And to that place a Story appertains,
Which, though it be ungarnish'd with events,
Is not unfit, I deem, for the fire-side,   20
Or for the summer shade. It was the first,
The earliest of those Tales that spake to me
Of Shepherds, dwellers in the Vallies, men
Whom I already lov'd, not verily
For their own sakes, but for the fields and hills   25
Where was their occupation and abode.
And hence this Tale, while I was yet a boy
Careless of books, yet having felt the power
Of Nature, by the gentle agency
Of natural objects led me on to feel   30
For passions that were not my own, and think
(At random and imperfectly indeed)
On man, the heart of man, and human life.[1]
Therefore, although it be a history
Homely and rude, I will relate the same   35
For the delight of a few natural hearts,
And with yet fonder feeling, for the sake
Of youthful Poets, who among these Hills
Will be my second Self when I am gone.

UPON the Forest-side in Grasmere Vale   40
There dwelt a Shepherd, Michael was his name,
An old man, stout of heart, and strong of limb.
His bodily frame had been from youth to age
Of an unusual strength: his mind was keen,
Intense and frugal, apt for all affairs,   45
And in his Shepherd's calling he was prompt
And watchful[2] more than ordinary men.
Hence he had learn'd the meaning of all winds,
Of blasts of every tone, and often-times

---

[1] Wordsworth here affirms his cardinal belief that love of nature promotes empathy and the philosophical reflectiveness that leads to wisdom.

[2] In part of *The Prelude* (1799. ii. 277) written the previous year. Wordsworth uses the same two adjectives to describe a baby's eager attentiveness to its mother.

When others heeded not. He heard the South   50
Make subterraneous music, like the noise
Of Bagpipers on distant Highland Hills.
The Shepherd, at such warning, of his flock
Bethought him, and he to himself would say,
'The Winds are now devising work for me!'   55
And truly at all times the storm, that drives
The Traveller to a shelter, summon'd him
Up to the mountains: he had been alone
Amid the heart of many thousand mists
That came to him and left him on the heights.   60
So liv'd he till his eightieth year was pass'd.
And grossly that man errs, who should suppose
That the green Valleys, and the Streams and Rocks
Were things indifferent to the Shepherd's thoughts.
Fields where with chearful spirits he had breath'd   65
The common air; the hills, which he so oft
Had climb'd with vigorous steps; which had impress'd
So many incidents upon his mind
Of hardship, skill or courage, joy or fear;
Which like a book preserv'd the memory   70
Of the dumb animals, whom he had sav'd,
Had fed or shelter'd, linking to such acts,
So grateful[1] in themselves, the certainty
Of honorable gains; these fields, these hills
Which were his living Being even more   75
Than his own Blood—what could they less? had lay'd
Strong hold on his Affections, were to him
A pleasurable feeling of blind love,
The pleasure which there is in life itself.

He had not pass'd his days in singleness.   80
He had a Wife, a comely matron, old
Though younger than himself full twenty years.
She was a Woman of a stirring life
Whose heart was in her house: two wheels she had
Of antique form, this large for spinning wool,   85
That small for flax, and if one wheel had rest,

[1] Gratifying: Michael took pleasure in these acts of kindness.

It was because the other was at work.[1]
The Pair had but one Inmate in their house,
An only Child, who had been born to them
When Michael telling o'er his years, began   90
To deem that he was old, in shepherd's phrase,
With one foot in the grave. This only Son
With two brave Sheep-dogs tried[2] in many a storm,
The one of an inestimable worth,
Made all their Household. I may truly say,   95
That they were as a proverb in the vale
For endless industry. When day was gone,
And from their occupations out of doors
The Son and Father were come home, even then
Their labour did not cease, unless when all   100
Turn'd to the cleanly Supper-board, and there
Each with a mess of pottage[3] and skimm'd milk,
Sate round their Basket pil'd with oaten cake
And their plain home-made cheese. Yet when their Meal
Was ended, LUKE (for so the Son was nam'd)[4]   105
And his old Father both betook themselves
To such convenient work, as might employ
Their hands by the fire-side; perhaps to card
Wool for the House-wife's spindle, or repair
Some injury done to sickle, flail, or scythe,   110
Or other implement of house or field.

Down from the ceiling, by the chimney's edge
Which in our antient uncouth[5] country style
Did with a huge Projection overbrow
Large space beneath, as duly as the light   115

[1] The household is thus dependent on the type of cottage industry which the Industrial Revolution would destroy.
[2] Tested and thus proved to be valuable.
[3] Portion of stew. This phrase was current in allusions to Genesis (25:29–34) where Esau, reckless with hunger, gives his birthright to his younger brother Jacob in exchange for 'a mess of pottage'. As well as suggesting the biblical simplicity of Michael's life, the phrase foreshadows Luke's unfilial recklessness.
[4] Luke's name, like his father's, has strong biblical associations.
[5] 'our . . . uncouth' contains a subtle note of defiance common in Wordsworth's expressions of solidarity with the rural poor.

Of day grew dim, the House-wife hung a Lamp,
An aged utensil, which had perform'd
Service beyond all others of its kind.
Early at evening did it burn and late,
Surviving Comrade of uncounted Hours   120
Which going by from year to year had found,
And left the Couple neither gay perhaps
Nor chearful, yet with objects and with hopes
Living a life of eager industry.
And now when Luke was in his eighteenth year,   125
There by the light of this old Lamp they sate,
Father and Son, while late into the night
The House-wife plied her own peculiar[1] work,
Making the Cottage through the silent hours
Murmur as with the sound of summer flies.   130
Not with a waste of words, but for the sake
Of pleasure, which I know that I shall give
To many living now, I of this Lamp
Speak thus minutely; for there are no few
Whose memories will bear witness to my Tale.   135
The Light was famous in its neighbourhood
And was a public Symbol of the life,
That thrifty Pair had liv'd. For as it chanc'd
Their Cottage on a plot of rising ground
Stood single, with large prospect North and South,   140
High into Easedale, up to Dunmal-Raise,
And Westward to the Village near the Lake.[2]
And from this constant light so regular
And so far seen, the House itself by all
Who dwelt within the limits of the Vale,   145
Both old and young, was nam'd The Evening Star.

Thus living on through such a length of years
The Shepherd if he lov'd himself must needs
Have lov'd his Helpmate; but to Michael's heart
This Son of his old age was yet more dear—   150
Effect which might perhaps have been produc'd
By that instinctive tenderness, the same

[1] Proper, appropriate (*not* strange).
[2] Grasmere.

Blind Spirit, which is in the blood of all,[1]
Or that a child more than all other gifts
Brings hope with it, and forward-looking thoughts   155
And stirrings of inquietude, when they[2]
By tendency of nature needs must fail.
From such and other causes to the thoughts
Of the old Man his only Son was now
The dearest object that he knew on earth.   160
Exceeding was the Love he bare to him,
His Heart and his Heart's Joy! For oftentimes
Old Michael, while he[3] was a Babe in arms,
Had done him female service, not alone
For dalliance[4] and delight, as is the use[5]   165
Of Fathers, but with patient mind enforc'd
To acts of tenderness; and he had rock'd
His cradle, with a woman's gentle hand.

And, in a later time, ere yet the Boy
Had put on Boy's attire, did Michael love,   170
Albeit of a stern unbending mind,
To have the young one in his sight, when he
Had work by his own door, or when he sate
With sheep before him on his Shepherd's stool[6]
Beneath that large old Oak, which near their door   175
Stood, and from its enormous breadth of shade,
Chosen for the Shearer's covert from the sun,
Thence in our rustic dialect was call'd
The CLIPPING TREE,[7] a name which yet it bears.
There, while they two were sitting in the shade,   180
With others round them, earnest all and blithe,

[1] Wordsworth insists on the universality of 'the essential passions of the heart'.
[2] Grammatically, the 'forward-looking thoughts'; but with a flicker of relevance to 'children'.
[3] Luke.
[4] Probably combining the senses of chatter and affectionate play.
[5] Custom.
[6] Wordsworth later revised these lines so as to eliminate the suggestion that the sheep were sitting on the stool.
[7] 'Clipping is the word used in the North of England for shearing.' (Wordsworth's note).

Would Michael exercise his heart with looks
Of fond correction and reproof bestow'd
Upon the Child, if he disturb'd the sheep
By catching at their legs, or with his shouts   185
Scar'd them, while they lay still beneath the Shears.

And when by Heaven's good grace the Boy grew up
A healthy Lad, and carried in his cheek
Two steady[1] roses that were five years old,
Then Michael from a winter coppice cut   190
With his own hand a sapling, which he hoop'd
With iron, making it throughout in all
Due requisites a perfect Shepherd's Staff,
And gave it to the Boy; wherewith equipp'd
He as a Watchman oftentimes was plac'd   195
At gate or gap to stem or turn the Flock,
And, to his office prematurely call'd
There stood the Urchin,[2] as you will divine,
Something between a hindrance and a help,
And for this cause not always I believe   200
Receiving from his Father hire[3] of praise
Though nought was left undone, which staff, or voice
Or looks or threatening gestures could perform.
But soon as Luke, now ten years old, could stand
Against the mountain blasts, and to the Heights,   205
Not fearing toil, nor length of weary ways,
He with his Father daily went, and they
Were as companions, why should I relate
That objects which the Shepherd lov'd before
Were dearer now? That from the Boy there came   210
Feelings and emanations,[4] things which were
Light to the sun and music to the wind,
And that the Old Man's Heart seem'd born again?[5]

[1] For Wordsworth a word with strong connotations of moral stability.

[2] A mischievous youngster, here used affectionately.

[3] Reward (for his 'work').

[4] Love-inspiring influences. The term was often used for the creative energies of God.

[5] An unmistakable echo of 'Except a man be born again, he cannot see the kingdom of God' (John 3:3).

Thus in his Father's sight the Boy grew up,
And now when he had reach'd his eighteenth year,   215
He was his comfort and his daily hope.

WHILE[1] this good household thus were living on
From day to day, to Michael's ear there came
Distressful tidings. Long before the time
Of which I speak, the Shepherd had been bound   220
In surety[2] for his Brother's Son, a man
Of an industrious life and ample means,
But unforeseen misfortunes suddenly
Had press'd upon him, and old Michael now
Was summon'd to discharge the forfeiture,[3]   225
A grievous penalty, but little less
Than half his substance. This unlook'd-for claim,
At the first hearing for a moment took
More hope out of his life than he supposed
That any old man ever could have lost.   230
As soon as he had gather'd so much strength
That he could look his trouble in the face,
It seem'd that his sole refuge was to sell
A portion of his patrimonial fields.[4]
Such was his first resolve; he thought again   235
And his heart fail'd him. 'Isabel,' said he,
Two evenings after he had heard the news,
'I have been toiling more than seventy years,
And in the open sunshine of God's love
Have we all lived, yet if these fields of ours   240
Should pass into a Stranger's hand, I think
That I could not lie quiet in my grave.
Our lot is a hard lot; the sun itself
Has scarcely been more diligent than I,
And I have lived to be a fool at last   245
To my own family. An evil Man

---

[1] Here begins what Wordsworth referred to privately as the 'second Part of the Poem'.
[2] i.e. had put up his own assets as collateral.
[3] Pay off the debt which he had insured.
[4] i.e. the land which Michael had inherited from his father.

That was,[1] and made an evil choice, if he
Were false to us; and if he were not false,
There are ten thousand to whom loss like this
Had been no sorrow. I forgive him; — but   250
'Twere better to be dumb than to talk thus.
When I began, my purpose was to speak
Of remedies and of a chearful hope.
Our Luke shall leave us, Isabel; the land
Shall not go from us, and it shall be free,[2]   255
He shall possess it, free as is the wind
That passes over it. We have, thou knowest,
Another kinsman, he will be our friend
In this distress. He is a prosperous man,
Thriving in trade, and Luke to him shall go   260
And with his Kinsman's help and his own thrift
He quickly will repair this loss, and then
May[3] come again to us. If here he stay,
What can be done? Where every one is poor
What can be gain'd?' At this the old man paus'd,   265
And Isabel sate silent, for her mind
Was busy, looking back into past times.
There's Richard Bateman, thought she to herself,
He was a parish Boy—At the church door
They made a gathering for him, shillings, pence,   270
And halfpennies, wherewith the Neighbours bought
A Basket, which they fill'd with Pedlar's wares,
And, with this basket on his arm the Lad
Went up to London, found a Master there
Who out of many chose the trusty Boy   275
To go and overlook his merchandise
Beyond the seas, where he grew wondrous rich,
And left estates and monies to the poor,
And at his birth-place built a Chapel, floor'd
With marble, which he sent from foreign Lands.   280
These thoughts and many others of like sort

[1] i.e. It would have been evil of his nephew to have dealt with Michael dishonestly.

[2] Freehold. Michael implicitly rejects the solution of mortgaging his land. which, unlike most Statesmen (Westmorland farmers) he owns outright.

[3] Eerily ambiguous: a) will be able to: b) might.

Pass'd quickly through the mind of Isabel
And her face brighten'd. The Old Man was glad
And thus resumed. 'Well! Isabel, this scheme
These two days has been meat and drink to me.   285
Far more than we have lost is left us yet.
—We have enough—I wish indeed that I
Were younger, but this hope is a good hope.
—Make ready Luke's best garments, of the best
Buy for him more, and let us send him forth   290
To-morrow, or the next day, or to-night,
—If he could go the Boy should go to-night.'

Here Michael ceas'd, and to the fields went forth
With a light heart. The Housewife for five days
Was restless morn and night, and all day long   295
Wrought on with her best fingers to prepare
Things needful for the journey of her Son.
But Isabel was glad when Sunday came
To stop her in her work:[1] for, when she lay
By Michael's side, she through the last two nights   300
Heard him, how he was troubled in his sleep;
And when they rose at morning she could see
That all his hopes were gone. That day at noon
She said to Luke while they two by themselves
Were sitting at the door, 'Thou must not go,   305
We have no other Child but thee to lose,
None to remember—do not go away,
For if thou leave thy Father he will die.'
The Lad made answer with a jocund voice,
And Isabel when she had told her fears,   310
Recover'd heart. That evening her best fare
Did she bring forth, and all together sate
Like happy people round a Christmas fire.

With daylight Isabel resumed her work,
And all the ensuing week the house appear'd   315
As cheerful as a grove in spring: at length
The expected letter from their Kinsman came

[1] By having them observe the Sabbath (a day of rest) Wordsworth indicates their piety.

With kind assurances that he would do
His utmost for the welfare of the Boy,
To which requests were added that forthwith   320
He might be sent to him. Ten times or more
The letter was read over, Isabel
Went forth to show it to the neighbours round,
Nor was there at that time on English Land
A prouder heart than Luke's. When Isabel   325
Had to her house returned, the Old Man said,
'He shall depart to-morrow.' To this word
The Housewife answered, talking much of things
Which, if at such short notice he should go,
Would surely be forgotten. But at length   330
She gave consent, and Michael was at ease.

Near the tumultuous brook of Green-head Gill
In that deep Valley Michael had designed
To build a Sheep-fold[1] and, before he heard
The tidings of his melancholy loss,   335
For this same purpose he had gathered up
A heap of stones, which close to the brook side
Lay thrown together, ready for the work.
With Luke that evening thitherward he walk'd;
And soon as they had reach'd the place he stopp'd   340
And thus the old Man spake to him: 'My Son,[2]
To-morrow thou wilt leave me; with full heart

I look upon thee, for thou art the same
That wert a promise to me ere thy birth,
And all thy life hast been my daily joy.   345
I will relate to thee some little part
Of our two histories; 'twill do thee good
When thou art from[3] me, even if I should speak
Of things thou canst not know of. —— After thou
First cam'st into the world, as it befalls   350

[1] 'an unroofed building of stone walls, with different divisions'
(Wordsworth's note).
[2] These two words are many times repeated in David's lament over his
dead son Absolom (2 Samuel 18:33), a passage that Wordsworth profoundly
admired.
[3] Away from.

To new-born infants, thou didst sleep away
Two days, and blessings from thy Father's tongue
Then fell upon thee. Day by day pass'd on,
And still I lov'd thee with encreasing love.
Never to living ear came sweeter sounds   355
Than when I heard thee by our own fire-side
First uttering without words a natural tune,
When thou, a feeding babe, didst in thy joy
Sing at thy Mother's breast. Month follow'd month,
And in the open fields my life was pass'd   360
And in the mountains, else I think that thou
Hadst been brought up upon thy father's knees.
—But we were playmates, Luke; among these hills,
As well thou know'st, in us the old and young
Have play'd together, nor with me didst thou   365
Lack any pleasure which a boy can know.'
Luke had a manly heart; but at these words
He sobb'd aloud; The old Man grasp'd his hand,
And said, 'Nay do not take it so—I see
That these are things of which I need not speak.   370
—Even to the utmost I have been to thee
A kind and a good Father: and herein
I but repay a gift which I myself
Receiv'd at others' hands, for, though now old
Beyond the common life of man, I still   375
Remember them who lov'd me in my youth.
Both of them sleep together: here they liv'd,
As all their Forefathers had done, and when
At length their time was come they were not loth
To give their bodies to the family mold.[1]   380
I wish'd that thou should'st live the life they liv'd.
But 'tis a long time to look back, my Son,
And see so little gain from sixty years.
These fields were burthen'd[2] when they came to me,
'Till I was forty years of age, not more   385
Than half of my inheritance was mine.

[1] The chief sense is 'earth-mould'. hence grave: but Wordsworth's
awareness of 'mould' in the sense of 'model' emerges in the next line.
[2] With restrictions on the terms of Michael's ownership.

I toil'd and toil'd; God bless'd me in my work
And 'till these three weeks past the land was free,
—It looks as if it never could endure
Another master. Heaven forgive me, Luke,   390
If I judge ill for thee, but it seems good
That thou should'st go.' At this the Old Man paus'd,
Then, pointing to the stones near which they stood,
Thus after a short silence, he resumed.
'This was a work for us; and now, my Son,   395
It is a work for me. But lay one stone,
Here lay it for me, Luke, with thine own hands.
I for the purpose brought thee to this place.
Nay, Boy, be of good hope:—we both may live
To see a better day: at eighty-four[1]   400
I still am strong and stout,—do thou thy part,
I will do mine.—I will begin again
With many tasks that were resigned to thee,
Up to the heights and in among the storms,
Will I without thee go again, and do   405
All works which I was wont to do alone,
Before I knew thy face—Heaven bless thee, Boy,
Thy heart these two weeks has been beating fast
With many hopes—it should be so—yes—yes—
I knew that thou could'st never have a wish   410
To leave me, Luke,—thou hast been bound to me
Only by links of love: when thou art gone,
What will be left to us!—But I forget
My purposes. Lay now the corner stone
As I requested, and hereafter, Luke,   415
When thou art gone away, should evil men
Be thy companions, let this Sheep-fold be
Thy anchor and thy shield;[2] amid all fear
And all temptation let it be to thee
An emblem of the life thy Fathers[3] liv'd,   420

[1] Luke, now 18, was therefore born when Michael was 66.
[2] The metaphors, and the mixing of them, are biblical. In Genesis
31:43–55, the covenant between Jacob and his father-in-law, Laban, is
similarly marked with a cairn.
[3] Forefathers.

Who, being innocent, did for that cause
Bestir them in good deeds. Now, fare thee well:
When thou return'st thou in this place wilt see
A work which is not here, a covenant[1]
'Twill be between us —— but whatever fate   425
Befall thee, I shall love thee to the last,
And bear thy memory with me to the grave.'

The Shepherd ended here; and Luke stoop'd down,
And, as his Father had requested, laid
The first stone of the Sheep-fold; at the sight   430
The Old Man's grief broke from him, to his heart
He press'd his Son, he kissed him and wept:
And to the house together they return'd.

Next morning, as had been resol'd, the Boy
Began his journey, and when he had reach'd   435
The public Way, he put on a bold face;
And all the Neighbours as he pass'd their doors
Came forth with wishes and with farewell prayers,
That follow'd him 'till he was out of sight.

A good report did from their Kinsman come   440
Of Luke and his well doing; and the Boy
Wrote loving letters full of wondrous news,
Which, as the Housewife phras'd it, were throughout
The prettiest letters that were ever seen.
Both parents read them with rejoicing hearts.   445
So, many months pass'd on: and once again
The shepherd went about his daily work
With confident and cheerful thoughts; and now
Sometimes when he could find a leisure hour
He to that valley took his way, and there   450
Wrought at the sheep-fold. Meantime Luke began

---

[1] (Mark of) a solemn agreement. The word is used generally throughout the Bible for 'agreements between God and man'. More specifically it denotes the ethical systems propounded by Moses and Christ (the 'Old' covenant and the 'New'). A leading characteristic of the New Covenant is its emphasis on unconditional love of the kind expressed by Michael for Luke.

To slacken in his duty, and, at length
He in the dissolute city[1] gave himself
To evil courses: ignominy and shame
Fell on him, so that he was driven at last   455
To seek a hiding-place beyond the seas.

There is a comfort in the strength of love;
'Twill make a thing endurable, which else
Would break the heart:—old Michael found it so.
I have convers'd with more than one who well   460
Remember the Old Man, and what he was
Years after he had heard this heavy news.
His bodily frame had been from youth to age
Of an unusual strength. Among the rocks
He went, and still look'd up upon the sun,   465
And listen'd to the wind, and as before,
Perform'd all kinds of labour for his sheep,
And for the land his small[2] inheritance.
And to that hollow Dell from time to time
Did he repair, to build the Fold of which   470
His flock had need. 'Tis not forgotten yet
The pity which was then in every heart
For the Old Man—and 'tis believ'd by all
That many and many a day he thither went,
And never lifted up a single stone.   475
There, by the Sheep-fold, sometimes was he seen
Sitting alone, with that his faithful Dog,
Then old, beside him, lying at his feet.
The length of full seven years from time to time,
He at the building of this sheep-fold wrought,   480
And left the work unfinish'd when he died.

Three years, or little more, did Isabel
Survive her Husband: at her death the estate
Was sold, and went into a Stranger's hand.
The Cottage which was nam'd the Evening Star   485

[1] Wordsworth does not shrink from a categorical denunciation of city-life.
[2] The greater part having now been forfeited.

Is gone, the ploughshare has been through the ground
On which it stood; great changes have been wrought
In all the neighbourhood, yet the Oak is left
That grew beside their Door; and the remains
Of the unfinished Sheep-fold may be seen   490
Beside the boisterous brook of Green-head Gill.

1800   1800

[My heart leaps up when I behold]

My heart leaps up when I behold
        A rainbow in the sky:
So was it when my life began;
So is it now I am a Man;
So be it when I shall grow old,   5
        Or let me die!
The Child is father of the Man;
And I could wish my days to be
Bound each to each by natural piety.

1802   1807

To H.C.,[1] Six Years Old

O Thou! whose fancies from afar are brought;
Who of thy words dost make a mock apparel,
And fittest to unutterable thought
The breeze-like motion and the self-born carol;[2]

---

[1] Hartley Coleridge (1796–1849), eldest son of S. T. Coleridge.
[2] Originally, a ring-dance with song; here, a joyful song with a hint of dancing.

Thou Faery[1] Voyager! that dost float 5
In such clear water, that thy Boat
May rather seem
To brood on air than on an earthly stream;
Suspended in a stream as clear as sky,
Where earth and heaven do make one imagery;[2] 10
O blessed Vision! happy Child!
Thou art so exquisitely wild,
I think of thee with many fears
For what may be thy lot in future years.[3]

I thought of times when Pain might be thy guest, 15
Lord of thy house and hospitality;
And Grief, uneasy Lover! never rest
But when she sate within the touch of thee.
Oh! too industrious folly!
Oh! vain and causeless melancholy! 20
Nature will either end thee quite;
Or, lengthening out thy season of delight,
Preserve for thee, by individual right,
A young Lamb's heart among the full-grown flocks.
What hast Thou to do with sorrow, 25
Or the injuries of tomorrow?
Thou art a Dew-drop, which the morn brings forth,
Not doom'd to jostle with unkindly shocks,
Or to be trail'd along the soiling earth;
A Gem that glitters while it lives, 30
And no forewarning gives;
But, at the touch of wrong, without a strife
Slips in a moment out of life.

1802–4   1807

---

[1] This spelling of 'fairy' indicates the imaginary world of Spenser's *The Faerie Queene* (1590–6), an epic romance in which the distinction between the ordinary and the divine is continually dissolved.

[2] Combination of pictorial images: picture.

[3] Wordsworth's fears proved just. Hartley's early promise was tragically unfulfilled.

Ode[1]

Paulò majora canamus[2]

There was a time when meadow, grove, and stream,
The earth, and every common sight,
      To me did seem
      Apparell'd in celestial light,
The glory and the freshness of a dream.   5
It is not now as it has been of yore;—
      Turn whereso'er I may,
      By night or day,
The things which I have seen I now can see no more.

      The Rainbow comes and goes,   10
      And lovely is the Rose,
      The Moon doth with delight
Look round her when the heavens are bare;
      Waters on a starry night
      Are beautiful and fair;   15
      The sunshine is a glorious birth;
      But yet I know, where'er I go,
That there hath pass'd away a glory from the earth.

Now, while the Birds thus sing a joyous song,
      And while the young Lambs bound   20
      As to the tabor's[3] sound,
To me alone there came a thought of grief:
A timely utterance gave that thought relief,
      And I again am strong:
The Cataracts[4] blow their trumpets from the steep;   25
No more shall grief of mine the season wrong;

[1] The final, and culminating, poem in *Poems in Two Volumes* (1807). A
subtitle, 'Intimations of Immortality from Recollections of Early Childhood' was
added in 1815. The poem is centrally concerned with 'an intimation or
assurance within us, that some part of our nature is imperishable'. ('Essay
upon Epitaphs.' 1810).
[2] 'Let us sing a somewhat loftier strain.' (Virgil *Eclogues* IV.i).
[3] A small drum, frequently mentioned in the Psalms.
[4] Waterfalls.

I hear the Echoes through the mountains throng,
The Winds come to me from the fields of sleep,[1]
    And all the earth is gay,
      Land and sea   30
    Give themselves up to jollity,
     And with the heart of May
    Doth every Beast keep holiday,
     Thou Child of Joy,
Shout round me, let me hear thy shouts, thou happy   35
                         Shepherd Boy!

Ye blessed Creatures, I have heard the call
    Ye to each other make; I see
The heavens laugh with you in your jubilee;[2]
    My heart is at your festival,
     My head hath its coronal,[3]   40
The fulness of your bliss, I feel—I feel it all.
    Oh evil day! if I were sullen
    While Earth herself is adorning,
     This sweet May-morning,
    And the Children are pulling   45
     On every side,
    In a thousand valleys far and wide,
    Fresh flowers; while the sun shines warm,
And the Babe leaps up on his mother's arm:—
    I hear, I hear, with joy I hear!   50
    —But there's a Tree, of many one,
A single Field which I have look'd upon,
Both of them speak of something that is gone:
    The Pansy at my feet
    Doth the same tale repeat: 55
Whither is fled the visionary gleam?
Where is it now, the glory and the dream?

[1] Richly ambiguous: a) the landscape has entered even my dreams; b) the winds at dusk or dawn are gentle from crossing sleepy fields; c) the winds carry gentle forebodings of a final rest.

[2] Time of celebration; but, in the strongly biblical context of this poem, the word is tinged with its original sense of a year when slaves were set free and property restored to its former owners (Leviticus 25:10).

[3] Circlet of gold, gems or flowers for crowning.

Our birth is but a sleep and a forgetting:
The Soul that rises with us, our life's Star,[1]
    Hath had elsewhere it's setting,   60
    And cometh from afar:
Not in entire forgetfulness,
And not in utter nakedness,
But trailing clouds of glory do we come
    From God, who is our home:[2]   65
Heaven lies about us in our infancy!
Shades of the prison-house[3] begin to close
    Upon the growing Boy,
But He beholds the light, and whence it flows,
    He sees it in his joy;   70
The Youth, who daily farther from the East
    Must travel, still is Nature's Priest,[4]
    And by the vision splendid
    Is on his way attended;
At length the Man perceives it die away,   75
And fade into the light of common day.

Earth fills her lap with pleasures of her own;
Yearnings she hath in her own natural kind,
And, even with something of a Mother's mind,
    And no unworthy aim,   80
  The homely Nurse doth all she can
To make her Foster-child, her Inmate[5] Man,
    Forget the glories he hath known,
And that imperial palace[6] whence he came.

Behold the Child among his new-born blisses,   85
A four year's[7] Darling of a pigmy size!
See, where 'mid work of his own hand he lies,

[1] Lodestar: that which gives direction and purpose to our lives.
[2] Wordsworth denied he was promoting belief in pre-existence. yet noted that 'the fall of Man presents an analogy in its favour. Accordingly, a pre-existent state has entered into the popular creeds of many nations.' (1843).
[3] The habits of perception which thwart our imaginative life.
[4] i.e. he demonstrates the presence of God in Nature (human and material).
[5] With a hint of the sense suggested by 'prison-house'.
[6] Heaven: God's empire; hence 'imperial'.
[7] Changed in 1815 to 'six years'.

Fretted by sallies[1] of his Mother's kisses,
With light upon him from his Father's eyes!
See, at his feet, some little plan or chart,   90
Some fragment from his dream of human life,
Shap'd by himself with newly-learned art;
      A wedding or a festival,
      A mourning or a funeral;
        And this hath now his heart,   95
      And unto this he frames his song:
        Then will he fit his tongue
To dialogues of business, love, or strife;
      But it will not be long
      Ere this be thrown aside,   100
      And with new joy and pride[2]
The little Actor cons another part;
Filling from time to time his 'humorous stage'[3]
With all the Persons, down to palsied Age,
That Life brings with her in her Equipage;[4]   105
      As if his whole vocation
      Were endless imitation.

Thou, whose exterior semblance doth belie
      Thy Soul's immensity;
Thou best Philosopher,[5] who yet dost keep   110
Thy heritage, thou Eye among the blind,
That, deaf and silent, read'st the eternal deep,
Haunted for ever by the eternal mind, —
      Mighty Prophet! Seer[6] blest!
      On whom those truths do rest,   115
Which we are toiling all our lives to find;
Thou, over whom thy Immortality

[1] Vexed by sudden 'assaults' of kissing.

[2] The word's current sense of 'innocent self-satisfaction' was in Wordsworth's time inevitably attended by the theological sense of 'ungodly presumption'.

[3] Quoted from Samuel Daniel (1563–1619). The idea is of a stage on which actors representing different 'humours' or temperaments might perform.

[4] Vaguely, apparatus; or, vividly, horse-drawn carriage.

[5] Possessor (and encourager) of wisdom.

[6] One who sees into spiritual mysteries.

... the Day, a Master o'er a Slave,
... resence which is not to be put by;
    To whom the grave   120
Is but a lonely bed without the sense or sight
    Of day or the warm light,
A place of thought where we in waiting lie;[2]
Thou little Child, yet glorious in the might
Of untam'd pleasures, on thy Being's height,   125
Why with such earnest pains dost thou provoke
The Years to bring the inevitable yoke,
Thus blindly with thy blessedness at strife?
Full soon thy Soul shall have her earthly freight,
And custom lie upon thee with a weight,   130
Heavy as frost, and deep almost as life!

    O joy! that in our embers
    Is something that doth live,
    That nature yet remembers
    What was so fugitive![3]   135
The thought of our past years in me doth breed
Perpetual benedictions:[4] not indeed
For that which is most worthy to be blest;
Delight and liberty, the simple creed
Of Childhood, whether fluttering or at rest,   140
With new-born hope for ever in his breast:—
    Not for these I raise
    The song of thanks and praise;
    But for those obstinate questionings
    Of sense and outward things,   145
    Fallings from us, vanishings;
    Blank misgivings of a Creature
Moving about in worlds not realiz'd,
High instincts before which our mortal Nature
Did tremble like a guilty Thing[5] surpriz'd: 150

[1] a) Lours; b) warms nurturingly, as a hen does eggs.
[2] Dorothy's journal describes the pleasure she and Wordsworth took in imagining themselves lying awake in a grave.
[3] i.e. that *human* nature can recall a state of being so fleeting ('fugitive').
[4] Thanksgivings.
[5] The ghost in *Hamlet* shrinks from the dawn 'like a guilty thing' (I.i.129).

But for those first affections,
Those shadowy recollections,
Which, be they what they may,
Are yet the fountain light of all our day,
Are yet a master light of all our seeing;   155
Uphold us,[1] cherish us, and make
Our noisy years seem moments in the being
Of the eternal Silence: truths that wake,
To perish never;
Which neither listlessness, nor mad endeavour,   160
Nor Man nor Boy,
Nor all that is at enmity with joy,
Can utterly abolish or destroy!
Hence in a season of calm weather,
Though inland far[2] we be,   165
Our Souls have sight of that immortal sea
Which brought us hither,
Can in a moment travel thither,
And see the Children sport upon the shore,
And hear the mighty waters rolling evermore.   170

Then, sing ye Birds, sing, sing a joyous song!
And let the young Lambs bound
As to the tabor's sound!
We in thought will join your throng,
Ye that pipe and ye that play,   175
Ye that through your hearts to-day
Feel the gladness of the May!
What though the radiance which was once so bright
Be now for ever taken from my sight,
Though nothing can bring back the hour   180
Of splendour in the grass, of glory in the flower;
We will grieve not, rather find
Strength in what remains behind,
In the primal sympathy[3]
Which having been must ever be,   185
In the soothing thoughts that spring

[1] i.e. *which* uphold us . . . etc.
[2] Far advanced into our earthly life and preoccupations.
[3] Feeling for human and material nature learnt in the earliest stages of life.

...man suffering,
... the faith that looks through death,
... years that bring the philosophic[1] mind.

And oh ye Fountains. Meadows, Hills, and Groves,   190
Think not of any severing of our loves!
Yet[2] in my heart of hearts I feel your might;
I only have relinquished one delight
To live beneath your more habitual sway.
I love the Brooks which down their channels fret,[3]   195
Even more than when I tripp'd lightly as they;
The innocent brightness of a new-born Day
            Is lovely yet;
The Clouds that gather round the setting sun
Do take a sober colouring from an eye   200
That hath kept watch o'er man's mortality;
Another race hath been, and other palms[4] are won.
Thanks to the human heart by which we live.
Thanks to its tenderness, its joys, and fears,
To me the meanest flower that blows can give   205
Thoughts that do often lie too deep for tears.

1802–4   1807

Resolution and Independence

There was a roaring in the wind all night;
The rain came heavily and fell in floods;
But now the sun is rising calm and bright;
The birds are singing in the distant woods;

[1] As generally in Wordsworth. 'wisely meditative.'
[2] Still.
[3] Move in agitated ripples: with an allusion to the sense of 'vex themselves'.
[4] Palm-leaves. used in classical and Christian times as symbols of victory.

Over his own sweet voice the Stock-dove broods,[1]   5
The Jay makes answer as the Magpie chatters;
And all the air is fill'd with pleasant noise of waters.[2]

All things that love the sun are out of doors;
The sky rejoices in the morning's birth;
The grass is bright with rain-drops; on the moors   10
The Hare is running races in her mirth;
And with her feet she from the plashy[3] earth
Raises a mist; which, glittering in the sun,
Runs with her all the way, wherever she doth run.

I was a Traveller then upon the moor;   15
I saw the Hare that rac'd about with joy;
I heard the woods, and distant waters, roar;
Or heard them not, as happy as a Boy:
The pleasant season did my heart employ:
My old remembrances went from me wholly;   20
And all the ways of men, so vain and melancholy.

But, as it sometimes chanceth, from the might
Of joy in minds that can no further go,
As high as we have mounted in delight
In our dejection do we sink as low,   25
To me that morning did it happen so;
And fears and fancies, thick upon me came;
Dim sadness, and blind thoughts, I knew not nor could name.

I heard the Sky-lark singing in the sky;
And I bethought me of the playful Hare: 30
Even such a happy Child of earth am I;
Even as these blissful Creatures do I fare;
Far from the world[4] I walk, and from all care;
But there may come another day to me,
Solitude, pain of heart, distress, and poverty.   35

[1] In the Preface of 1815, Wordsworth draws attention to the metaphor of
incubation in 'broods'.
[2] In Wordsworth's pronunciation a perfect rhyme.
[3] Dotted with puddles: marshy.
[4] In the biblical sense of the place where secular concerns are paramount.

My whole life I have liv'd in pleasant thought,
As if life's business were a summer mood;
As if all needful things would come unsought
To genial[1] faith, still rich in genial good;
But how can He expect that others should   40
Build for him, sow for him, and at his call
Love him, who for himself will take no heed at all?

I thought of Chatterton,[2] the marvellous Boy,
The sleepless Soul that perish'd in his pride;
Of Him[3] who walk'd in glory and in joy   45
Behind his plough, upon the mountain-side:
By our own spirits are we deified;
We Poets in our youth begin in gladness;
But thereof comes in the end despondency and madness.

Now, whether it were by peculiar[4] grace,   50
A leading from above, a something given,
Yet it befel, that, in this lonely place,
When up and down my fancy thus was driven,
When I with these untoward thoughts had striven,
I saw a Man before me unawares: 55
The oldest Man he seemed that ever wore grey hairs.

My course I stopped as soon as I espied
The Old Man in that naked wilderness:
Close by a Pond, upon the further side,
He stood alone: a minute's space I guess   60
I watch'd him, he continuing motionless:
To the Pool's further margin then I drew;
He being all the while before me full in view.

As a huge Stone is sometimes seen to lie
Couch'd on the bald top of an eminence;   65

[1] a) innate; b) cheerful.
[2] Thomas Chatterton (1752–70) committed suicide and became an archetype of neglected genius. His *Excellent Ballad of Charitie* has the same stanza form as 'Resolution and Independence'.
[3] Robert Burns (1759–96): a major influence on Wordsworth's lyrics and poetic theory.
[4] Special either in its nature, or in being bestowed uniquely on himself.

Wonder to all who do the same espy
By what means it could thither come, and whence;
So that it seems a thing endued with sense:
Like a Sea-beast crawl'd forth, which on a shelf
Of rock or sand reposeth, there to sun itself.　　　　　70

Such seem'd this Man,[1] not all alive nor dead,
Nor all asleep; in his extreme old age:
His body was bent double, feet and head
Coming together in their pilgrimage;
As if some dire constraint of pain, or rage　　　　　75
Of sickness felt by him in times long past,
A more than human weight upon his frame had cast.

Himself he propped, his body, limbs, and face,
Upon a long grey Staff of shaven wood:
And, still as I drew near with gentle pace,　　　　　80
Upon the little pond or moorish flood[2]
Motionless as a Cloud the old Man stood;
That heareth not the loud winds when they call;
And moveth all together, if it move at all.

At length, himself unsettling, he the Pond　　　　　85
Stirred with his Staff, and fixedly did look
Upon the muddy water, which he conn'd,[3]
As if he had been reading in a book:
And now such freedom as I could I took;
And, drawing to his side, to him did say,　　　　　90
'This morning gives us promise of a glorious day.'

A gentle answer did the Old Man make,
In courteous speech which forth he slowly drew:
And him with further words I thus bespake,
'What kind of work is that which you pursue?　　　　　95
This is a lonesome place for one like you.'

---

[1] In the 1815 Preface Wordsworth quotes this sequence of comparisons (stone – sea-beast – Man) as illustrating 'the conferring, the abstracting, and the modifying powers of the Imagination'.
[2] Patch of boggy water, such as might be found on a moor.
[3] Perused.

He answer'd me with pleasure and surprise;
And there was, while he spake, a fire about his eyes.

His words came feebly, from a feeble chest,
But each in solemn order follow'd each,   100
With something of a lofty utterance drest;
Choice word, and measured phrase; above the reach
Of ordinary men; a stately speech!
Such as grave Livers[1] do in Scotland use,
Religious men, who give to God and Man their dues.   105

He told me that he to this Pond had come
To gather Leeches, being old and poor:
Employment hazardous and wearisome!
And he had many hardships to endure:
From Pond to Pond he roam'd, from moor to moor,   110
Housing, with God's good help, by choice or chance:
And in this way he gain'd an honest maintenance.

The Old Man still stood talking by my side;
But now his voice to me was like a stream
Scarce heard; nor word from word could I divide;   115
And the whole Body of the Man did seem
Like one whom I had met with in a dream;
Or like a Man from some far region sent,
To give me human strength, and strong admonishment.[2]

My former thoughts return'd: the fear that kills;   120
And hope that is unwilling to be fed;
Cold, pain, and labour, and all fleshly ills;
And mighty Poets in their misery dead.
And now, not knowing what the Old Man had said,
My question eagerly did I renew,   125
'How is it that you live, and what is it you do?'

He with a smile did then his words repeat;
And said, that, gathering Leeches, far and wide
He travelled; stirring thus about his feet

[1] An obsolete usage, meaning simply, 'those who live gravely'.
[2] Admonition: here, specifically, spiritual guidance.

The waters of the Ponds where they abide.   130
'Once I could meet with them on every side;
But they have dwindled long by slow decay;
Yet still I persevere, and find them where I may.'

While he was talking thus, the lonely place,
The Old Man's shape, and speech, all troubled me: 135
In my mind's eye I seem'd to see him pace
About the weary moors continually,
Wandering about alone and silently.
While I these thoughts within myself pursued,
He, having made a pause, the same discourse renewed.   140

And soon with this he other matter blended,
Chearfully uttered, with demeanour kind,
But stately in the main; and when he ended,
I could have laughed myself to scorn to find
In that decrepit Man so firm a mind.   145
'God,' said I, 'be my help and stay[1] secure;
I'll think of the Leech-gatherer on the lonely moor.'

1802   1807

[The world is too much with us]

The world[2] is too much with us; late and soon,
Getting and spending, we lay waste our powers:
Little we see in nature that is ours;
We have given our hearts away, a sordid boon![3]
This Sea that bares her bosom to the moon;   5
The Winds that will be howling at all hours
And are up-gathered now like sleeping flowers;

[1] Grammatically ambiguous: a) as noun = prop. b) as verb = remain.
[2] Here in the Christian sense of 'secular concerns at odds with spiritual welfare'.
[3] A gift; 'sordid' because the hearts are, in Wordsworth's view, depraved.

For this, for every thing, we are out of tune;
It moves us not. Great God! I'd rather be
A Pagan[1] suckled in a creed outworn;   10
So might I, standing on this pleasant lea,
Have glimpses that would make me less forlorn;
Have sight of Proteus[2] coming from the sea;
Or hear old Triton[3] blow his wreathed horn.

1802–4   1807

Composed upon Westminster Bridge,
Sept. 3, 1803

Earth has not any thing to shew more fair:
Dull would he be of soul who could pass by
A sight so touching in its majesty:
This City now doth like a garment, wear
The beauty of the morning; silent, bare,   5
Ships, towers, domes, theatres, and temples lie
Open unto the fields, and to the sky;
All bright and glittering in the smokeless air.
Never did sun more beautifully steep
In his first splendour, valley, rock, or hill;   10
Ne'er saw I, never felt, a calm so deep!
The river glideth at his own sweet will:
Dear God! the very houses seem asleep;
And all that mighty heart is lying still!

1802   1807

[1] Pagans differ from atheists in having a lively sense of the supernatural.
[2] In Greek myth, a prophetic sea-god able to change shape instantly.
[3] A sea-god with a man's torso, a fish's tail and a shell-horn.

[It is a beauteous Evening, calm and free]

It is a beauteous Evening, calm and free;
The holy time is quiet as a Nun
Breathless with adoration; the broad sun
Is sinking down in its tranquillity;
The gentleness of heaven is on the Sea: 5
Listen! the mighty Being is awake
And doth with his eternal motion make
A sound like thunder—everlastingly.
Dear Child! dear Girl! that walkest with me here,
If thou appear'st untouched by solemn thought,   10
Thy nature is not therefore less divine:
Thou liest in Abraham's bosom[1] all the year;
And worshipp'st at the Temple's inner shrine,[2]
God being with thee when we know it not.

1802   1807

To Toussaint L'ouverture[3]

Toussaint, the most unhappy Man of Men!
Whether the rural Milk-maid by her Cow
Sing in thy hearing, or thou liest now
Pillowed in some deep dungeon's earless den,
O miserable Chieftain! where and when   5
Wilt thou find patience! Yet die not; do thou
Wear rather in thy bonds a chearful brow:
Though fallen Thyself, never to rise again,
Live, and take comfort. Thou hast left behind
Powers that will work for thee; air, earth, and skies;   10

[1] Heaven, a place of rest for blessed souls (Luke 16:23).
[2] Its holiest part.
[3] Son of a negro slave: led insurrection in San Domingo against the whites
(1791); made governor of Haiti (1801). Following Napoleon's edict
re-establishing slavery (1801), taken to Paris, where he died in prison (1803).
His story gave a vital impulse to the anti-slavery movement.

There's not a breathing of the common wind
That will forget thee; thou hast great allies;
Thy friends are exultations, agonies,
And love, and Man's unconquerable mind.

1802   1803

Written in London, September, 1802[1]

O Friend! I know not which way I must look
For comfort, being, as I am, opprest
To think that now our Life is only drest
For shew; mean handywork of craftsman, cook,
Or groom![2] We must run glittering like a Brook   5
In the open sunshine, or we are unblest:
The wealthiest man among us is the best:[3]
No grandeur now in nature or in book
Delights us. Rapine,[4] avarice, expence,
This is idolatry; and these we adore: 10
Plain living and high thinking are no more:
The homely beauty of the good old cause
Is gone; our peace, our fearful innocence,
And pure religion breathing household laws.

1802   1807

[1] In 1802, having just returned from France. Wordsworth was struck 'with
the vanity and parade of our own country, especially in great towns and
cities . . .'
[2] Presumably alluding to the use of horses as status-symbols.
[3] Ironic.
[4] Strictly, 'seizing property by force'; hence materialistic self-indulgence.

London, 1802

Milton![1] thou should'st be living at this hour:
England hath need of thee: she is a fen
Of stagnant waters: altar, sword and pen,
Fireside, the heroic wealth of hall and bower,
Have forfeited their ancient English dower[2]   5
Of inward happiness. We are selfish men;
Oh! raise us up, return to us again;
And give us manners, virtue, freedom, power.
Thy soul was like a Star and dwelt apart:
Thou hadst a voice whose sound was like the sea;   10
Pure as the naked heavens, majestic, free,
So didst thou travel on life's common way,
In chearful godliness; and yet thy heart
The lowliest duties on itself did lay.

1802   1807

[She was a Phantom of delight]

She was a Phantom of delight[3]
When first she gleam'd upon my sight;
A lovely Apparition, sent
To be a moment's ornament;[4]
Her eyes as stars of Twilight fair;   5
Like Twilight's, too, her dusky hair;
But all things else about her drawn
From May-time and the cheerful Dawn;

[1] John Milton (1608–74). One of the four poets most revered by
Wordsworth (the others being Chaucer, Spenser and Shakespeare).
[2] Traditional accompaniment.
[3] Wordsworth is quoted as saying the poem was about his wife.
[4] Something which confers beauty or distinction (on a moment).

A dancing Shape, an Image gay,
To haunt, to startle, and way-lay.   10

I saw her upon nearer view,
A Spirit, yet a Woman too!
Her household motions light and free,
And steps of virgin liberty;[1]
A countenance in which did meet   15
Sweet records,[2] promises as sweet;
A Creature not too bright or good
For human nature's daily food;
For transient sorrows, simple wiles,
Praise, blame, love, kisses, tears, and smiles.   20

And now I see with eye serene
The very pulse of the machine,[3]
A Being breathing thoughtful breath,
A Traveller betwixt life and death;
The reason firm, the temperate will,   25
Endurance, foresight, strength, and skill;
A perfect Woman, nobly planned,
To warn, to comfort, and command;
And yet a Spirit still, and bright
With something of angelic light.   30

1803–4   1807

[I wandered lonely as a Cloud]

I wandered lonely as a Cloud
That floats on high o'er Vales and Hills,
When all at once I saw a crowd
A host of dancing Daffodils;
Along the Lake, beneath the trees,   5
Ten thousand dancing in the breeze.

---

[1] Spontaneity in a young woman arising from purity of heart.
[2] Accounts of past behaviour.
[3] Originally, any combination of parts, human or otherwise.

The waves beside them danced, but they
Outdid the sparkling waves in glee: –
A Poet could not but be gay,
In such a laughing company: 10
I gaz'd—and gaz'd—but little thought
What wealth the shew to me had brought:

For oft, when on my couch I lie
In vacant or in pensive mood,
They flash upon that inward eye   15
Which is the bliss of solitude,[1]
And then my heart with pleasure fills,
And dances with the Daffodils.

1804–7   1807

Elegiac Stanzas, Suggested by a Picture of Peele Castle, in a Storm, painted by Sir George Beaumont

I was thy Neighbour once, thou rugged Pile![2]
Four summer weeks I dwelt in sight of thee:
I saw thee every day; and all the while
Thy Form was sleeping on a glassy sea.

So pure the sky, so quiet was the air!   5
So like, so very like, was day to day!
Whene'er I look'd, thy Image still was there;
It trembled, but it never pass'd away.

How perfect was the calm! it seemed no sleep;

[1] Ll. 15–16, which Wordsworth considered the best in the poem, were written by his wife.

[2] A big, impressive building. Peele Castle is near Barrow-in-Furness, Cumbria.

No mood, which season takes away, or brings: 10
I could have fancied that the mighty Deep
Was even the gentlest of all gentle Things.

Ah! THEN, if mine had been the Painter's hand,
To express what then I saw; and add the gleam,
The light that never was, on sea or land,   15
The consecration, and the Poet's dream;

I would have planted thee, thou hoary Pile!
Amid a world how different from this![1]
Beside a sea that could not cease to smile;
On tranquil land, beneath a sky of bliss: 20

Thou[2] shouldst have seem'd a treasure-house, a mine
Of peaceful years; a chronicle of heaven:—
Of all the sunbeams that did ever shine
The very sweetest had to thee been given.

A Picture had it been of lasting ease,   25
Elysian[3] quiet, without toil or strife;
No motion but the moving tide, a breeze,
Or merely silent Nature's breathing life.

Such, in the fond[4] delusion of my heart,
Such Picture would I at that time have made: 30
And seen the soul of truth in every part;
A faith, a trust, that could not be betrayed.

So once it would have been,—'tis so no more;
I have submitted to a new controul:
A power is gone, which nothing can restore;   35
A deep distress[5] hath humaniz'd my Soul.

Not for a moment could I now behold

---

[1] This world in general. rather than the specific locality of Peele Castle.
[2] The castle.
[3] As of Elysium: in Greek mythology home of the blessed dead.
[4] Foolishly trusting and affectionate.
[5] The death by drowning of Wordsworth's brother John. 6 February 1805.

A smiling sea and be what I have been:
The feeling of my loss will ne'er be old;
This, which I know, I speak with mind serene.   40

Then, Beaumont,[1] Friend! who would have been the Friend,
If he had lived, of Him whom I deplore,[2]
This Work of thine I blame not, but commend;
This sea in anger, and that dismal shore.

Oh 'tis a passionate Work!—yet wise and well;   45
Well chosen is the spirit that is here;
That Hulk[3] which labours in the deadly swell,
This rueful sky, this pageantry[4] of fear!

And this huge Castle, standing here sublime,
I love to see the look with which it braves,   50
Cased in the unfeeling armour of old time,
The light'ning, the fierce wind, and trampling waves.

Farewell, farewell the Heart that lives alone,
Housed in a dream, at distance from the Kind![5]
Such happiness, wherever it be known,   55
Is to be pitied; for 'tis surely blind.

But welcome fortitude, and patient chear,
And frequent sights of what is to be borne!
Such sights, or worse, as are before me here.—[6]
Not without hope we suffer and we mourn.   60

1806   1807

---

[1] Sir George Beaumont (1753–1827), painter, was Wordsworth's friend and patron.
[2] Lament.
[3] A large ship, depicted in Beaumont's painting.
[4] Symbolic representation.
[5] (The bulk of) humankind; perhaps also, 'the regular course of things'.
[6] In the picture.

The Solitary Reaper

Behold her, single in the field,
Yon solitary Highland Lass!
Reaping and singing by herself;
Stop here, or gently pass!
Alone she cuts and binds the grain,   5
And sings a melancholy strain;
O listen! for the Vale profound
Is overflowing with the sound.

No Nightingale did ever chaunt[1]
So sweetly to reposing bands   10
Of Travellers in some shady haunt,
Among Arabian sands:
No sweeter voice was ever heard
In spring-time from the Cuckoo-bird,
Breaking the silence of the seas   15
Among the farthest Hebrides.

Will no one tell me what she sings? —[2]
Perhaps the plaintive numbers[3] flow
For old, unhappy, far-off things,
And battles long ago: 20
Or is it some more humble lay,
Familiar matter of to-day?
Some natural sorrow, loss, or pain,
That has been, and may be again!

Whate'er the theme, the Maiden sang   25
As if her song could have no ending;
I saw her singing at her work,
And o'er the sickle bending;

[1] An old spelling and pronunciation of 'chant'.
[2] Wilkinson describes the girl as singing in Erse (Highland Gaelic).
[3] Musical phrases.

I listen'd till I had my fill:
And, as I mounted up the hill,   30
The music in my heart I bore,
Long after it was heard no more.

1805   1807

Characteristics of a Child three Years old[1]

Loving she is, and tractable, though wild;
And Innocence hath privilege in her
To dignify arch looks and laughing eyes;
And feats of cunning; and the pretty round
Of trespasses, affected to provoke   5
Mock-chastisement and partnership in play.
And, as a faggot[2] sparkles on the hearth,
Not less if unattended and alone
Than when both young and old sit gathered round
And take delight in its activity;   10
Even so this happy Creature of herself
Is all sufficient; solitude to her
Is blithe society, who fills the air
With gladness and involuntary songs
Light are her sallies[3] as the tripping Fawn's   15
Forth-startled, from the fern where she lay couched;
Unthought-of, unexpected as the stir
Of the soft breeze ruffling the meadow flowers;
Or from before it chasing wantonly[4]

[1] Described by Wordsworth in 1843 as a 'Picture of my Daughter
Catharine, who died the year after' (4 June 1812, aged 3).
[2] Bundle of sticks, chiefly for burning on domestic fires.
[3] Literally, 'leaps', but 'playful movements' generally.
[4] Mischievously; in a free, uncontrolled way.

The many-coloured images impressed[1]   20
Upon the bosom of a placid lake.

1811–14   1815

[Surprized by joy—impatient as the Wind]

Surprized by joy—impatient as the Wind
I wished to share the transport—Oh! with whom
But Thee,[2] long buried in the silent Tomb,
That spot which no vicissitude[3] can find?
Love, faithful love recalled thee to my mind—   5
But how could I forget thee?—Through what power,
Even for the least division of an hour,
Have I been so beguiled as to be blind
To my most grievous loss?—That thought's return
Was the worst pang that sorrow ever bore,   10
Save one, one only, when I stood forlorn,
Knowing my heart's best treasure was no more;
That neither present time, nor years unborn
Could to my sight that heavenly face restore.

1813–14   1815

[1] Imparted to, as if by pressure.
[2] In 1843 Wordsworth said that the poem was inspired by his daughter
Catharine, who had died some two years before he wrote it.
[3] Change (good or bad) of circumstances.

Conclusion[1]

I thought of Thee, my partner and my guide,
As being past away.—Vain sympathies!
For, *backward*, Duddon! as I cast my eyes,
I see what was, and is, and will abide;
Still glides the Stream, and shall for ever glide;   5
The Form remains, the Function never dies;
While *we*, the brave, the mighty, and the wise,
We Men, who in our morn of youth defied
The elements, must vanish;—be it so!
Enough, if something from our hands have power   10
To live, and act, and serve the future hour;
And if, as tow'rd the silent tomb we go,
Thro' love, thro' hope, and faith's transcendent dower,
We feel that we are greater than we know.

1818–20   1820

Airey-Force Valley[2]

—— Not a breath of air
Ruffles the bosom of this leafy glen.
From the brook's margin, wide around, the trees
Are stedfast as the rocks; the brook itself,
Old as the hills that feed it from afar,   5
Doth rather deepen than disturb the calm
Where all things else are still and motionless.
And yet, even now, a little breeze, perchance
Escaped from boisterous winds that rage without,
Has entered, by the sturdy oaks unfelt,   10

---

[1] The last in a sequence of 34 sonnets published as *The River Duddon*.
[2] Airey – or more usually 'Aira' – force is a mountain 'brook' in the Lake District. with many quiet reaches among its waterfalls.

But to its gentle touch how sensitive
Is the light ash! that, pendent from the brow
Of yon dim cave, in seeming silence makes
A soft eye-music of slow-waving boughs,
Powerful almost as vocal harmony   15
To stay the wanderer's steps and soothe his thoughts.

1835   1842

Extempore Effusion upon the Death of James Hogg[1]

When first, descending from the moorlands,
I saw the Stream of Yarrow glide
Along a bare and open valley,
The Ettrick Shepherd[2] was my guide.

When last along its banks I wandered,   5
Through groves that had begun to shed
Their golden leaves upon the pathways,
My steps the border-minstrel[3] led.

The mighty Minstrel breathes no longer,
'Mid mouldering ruins low he lies;   10
And death upon the braes of Yarrow,[4]
Has closed the Shepherd-poet's eyes:

[1] 'These verses were written extempore, immediately after reading a notice of the Ettrick Shepherd's death in the Newcastle paper.' (Wordsworth).

[2] James Hogg (1770–1835). Wordsworth's sense of mortality may have been quickened by the fact that he and Hogg had been born in the same year.

[3] Sir Walter Scott (1771–1832), formerly renowned no less for his poetry than his novels.

[4] 'The Braes [steep valley hillsides] of Yarrow' is a famous ballad by John Logan (1747–88).

Nor has the rolling year twice measured,
From sign to sign, its stedfast course,
Since every mortal power of Coleridge[1]   15
Was frozen at its marvellous source;

The rapt One, of the godlike forehead,
The heaven-eyed creature sleeps in earth:
And Lamb, the frolic and the gentle,[2]
Has vanished from his lonely hearth.   20

Like clouds that rake the mountain-summits,
Or waves that own no curbing hand,
How fast has brother followed brother,
From sunshine to the sunless land!

Yet I, whose lids from infant slumbers   25
Were earlier raised,[3] remain to hear
A timid voice, that asks in whispers,
'Who next will drop and disappear?'

Our haughty life is crowned with darkness,
Like London with its own black wreath,   30
On which with thee, O Crabbe![4] forth-looking,
I gazed from Hampstead's breezy heath.

As if but yesterday departed,
Thou too art gone before; but why,
O'er ripe fruit, seasonably gathered,   35
Should frail survivors heave a sigh?

Mourn rather for that holy Spirit,
Sweet as the spring, as ocean deep;
For Her who, ere her summer faded,
Has sunk into a breathless sleep.[5]   40

[1] Samuel Taylor Coleridge (1772–1834), once Wordsworth's closest friend.
[2] Charles Lamb (1775–1834), who never married.
[3] Wordsworth was born earlier than everyone named here except Crabbe and Hogg.
[4] George Crabbe (1754–1832).
[5] Felicia Hemans (1793–1835), minor poet whom Wordsworth befriended.

No more of old romantic sorrows,
For slaughtered Youth or love-lorn Maid!
With sharper grief is Yarrow smitten,
And Ettrick mourns with her their Poet dead.

1835   1835

[Yes! thou art fair, yet be not moved]

Yes! thou art fair, yet be not moved
    To scorn the declaration,
That sometimes I in thee have loved
    My fancy's own creation.

Imagination needs must stir;   5
    Dear Maid, this truth believe,
Minds that have nothing to confer
    Find little to perceive.

Be pleased that nature made thee fit
    To feed my heart's devotion,   10
By laws to which all Forms submit
    In sky, air, earth, and ocean.

1845   1845

Poems published after Wordsworth's death

from [*The Prelude*][1]
i) The stolen boat (1805, i. 352–428)

    The mind of man is framed even like the breath
And harmony of music. There is a dark
Invisible workmanship that reconciles
Discordant elements, and makes them move   355
In one society. Ah me! that all
The terrors, all the early miseries,
Regrets, vexations, lassitudes, that all
The thoughts and feelings which have been infus'd
Into my mind should ever have made up   360
The calm existence that is mine when I
Am worthy of myself. Praise to the end!
Thanks likewise for the means! But I believe
That Nature, oftentimes, when she would frame
A favor'd Being, from his earliest dawn   365
Of infancy doth open out the clouds,
As at the touch of lightning, seeking him
With gentlest visitation: not the less,
Though haply aiming at the self-same end,
Does it delight her sometimes to employ   370
Severer interventions, ministry
More palpable,[2] and so she dealt with me.
    One evening (surely I was led by her)

---

[1] This title was supplied by Mary Wordsworth. Wordsworth himself
generally referred to the poem as 'the Poem to Coleridge'. Work on *The Prelude*
occupied him throughout his poetic career. The earliest-known passage,
beginning 'Was it for this' was composed in 1798, but was swiftly expanded
into the two-part *Prelude* of 1799. By 1804 this had grown into a poem of
five books, which by the following year had itself given rise to a thirteen-book
version. This 1805 version remained relatively stable, though it was subjected
to extensive revision before the first and posthumous publication of *The Prelude*
(by now in fourteen books) in July 1850. The following extracts are taken
from the version of 1805, for reasons explained in the Note on Texts. Line
numbers are those of that version.

[2] Able to be felt, as if by touch.

I went alone into a Shepherd's Boat,
A Skiff,[1] that to a Willow tree was tied   375
Within a rocky Cave, its usual home.
'Twas by the Shores of Patterdale, a Vale
Wherein I was a Stranger, thither come,
A School-boy Traveller, at the Holidays.
Forth rambled from the Village Inn alone   380
No sooner had I sight of this small Skiff,
Discover'd thus by unexpected chance,
Than I unloos'd her tether and embark'd.
The moon was up, the Lake was shining clear
Among the hoary[2] mountains: from the Shore   385
I push'd, and struck the oars and struck again
In cadence,[3] and my little Boat mov'd on
Even like a man who walks with stately step
Though bent on speed. It was an act of stealth
And troubled pleasure: nor without the voice   390
Of mountain echoes did my Boat move on,
Leaving behind her still[4] on either side
Small circles glittering idly in the moon,
Until they melted all into one track
Of sparkling light. A rocky steep uprose   395
Above the Cavern of the willow-tree,
And now, as suited one who proudly row'd
With his best skill, I fix'd a steady view
Upon the top of that same craggy ridge,
The bound of the horizon, for behind   400
Was nothing but the stars and the grey sky.
She was an elfin Pinnace;[5] lustily[6]
I dipp'd my oars into the silent Lake,
And, as I rose upon the stroke, my Boat
Went heaving through the water, like a Swan,   405
When from behind that craggy Steep, till then
The bound of the horizon, a huge Cliff,

---

[1] Small boat for a single rower.
[2] Frosty: hence indicating that it was the Christmas holidays.
[3] Rhythm: regular, measured movement.
[4] With an equivocation between the senses 'continually' and 'motionlessly'.
[5] In his excited imagination, the skiff became a small ship of elf-like charm.
[6] Zestfully.

As if with voluntary power instinct,[1]
Uprear'd its head: I struck, and struck again,
And, growing still in stature, the huge Cliff   410
Rose up between me and the stars, and still,
With measur'd motion, like a living thing
Strode after me. With trembling hands I turn'd,
And through the silent water stole my way
Back to the Cavern of the Willow-tree.   415
There in her mooring-place I left my Bark,[2]
And through the meadows homeward went with grave
And serious thoughts: and after I had seen
That spectacle, for many days my brain
Work'd with a dim and undetermin'd sense   420
Of unknown modes of being: in my thoughts
There was a darkness, call it solitude,
Or blank desertion, no familiar shapes
Of hourly objects, images of trees,
Of sea, or sky, no colours of green fields;   425
But huge and mighty forms that do not live
Like living men mov'd slowly through my mind
By day, and were the trouble of my dreams.

1798–1805   1926

ii) 'Bless'd the infant Babe' (1805, ii. 203–80)

Those incidental charms which first attach'd
My heart to rural objects, day by day
Grew weaker, and I hasten on to tell   205
How Nature, intervenient till this time
And secondary, now at length was sought
For her own sake. But who shall parcel out
His intellect, by geometric rules,
Split like a province, into round and square?   210
Who knows the individual hour in which
His habits were first sown, even as a seed,

---

[1] As if animated by a will of its own.
[2] The word is frequent in older poetry for a large boat. Indulgently ironic.

Who that shall point, as with a wand,[1] and say,
'This portion of the river of my mind
Came from yon fountain'?[2] Thou, my Friend![3] art one   215
More deeply read in thy own thoughts; to thee
Science[4] appears but, what in truth she is,
Not as our glory and our absolute boast,
But as a succedaneum, and a prop
To our infirmity. Thou art no slave   220
Of that false secondary power[5] by which,
In weakness we create distinctions, then
Believe our puny boundaries are things
Which we perceive, and not which we have made.
To thee, unblinded by these outward shows,   225
The unity of all has been reveal'd;
And thou wilt doubt with me,[6] less aptly skilled
Than many are to class the cabinet
Of their sensations,[7] and, in voluble phrase,
Run through the history and birth of each,   230
As of a single independent thing.
Hard task to analyse a soul, in which
Not only general habits and desires,
But each most obvious and particular thought,
Not in a mystical and idle[8] sense,   235
But in the words of reason[9] deeply weigh'd,
Hath no beginning.

                    Bless'd the infant Babe,
(For with my best conjectures I would trace
The progress of our being) blest the Babe,
Nurs'd in his Mother's arms, the Babe who sleeps   240
Upon his Mother's breast, who, when his soul

[1] Magic wand or teacher's pointing-stick.
[2] Tributary stream.
[3] Coleridge.
[4] Learning in general, *not* the natural sciences.
[5] Alludes to Coleridge's distinction between 'Reason' (intuition) and 'Understanding' (deduction), the latter being 'secondary'.
[6] Share my doubts.
[7] Mocks the idea of labelling 'sensations' like items in a display-case.
[8] Worthless.
[9] In the sense of intuition, rather than deduction.

Claims manifest kindred with an earthly soul,[1]
Doth gather passion from his Mother's eye!
Such feelings pass into his torpid life
Like an awakening breeze, and hence his mind,   245
Even in the first trial of its powers,
Is prompt and watchful, eager to combine
In one appearance all the elements
And parts of the same object, else detached
And loth to coalesce.[2] Thus day by day,   250
Subjected to the discipline of love,
His organs and recipient faculties
Are quicken'd, are more vigorous, his mind spreads,
Tenacious of the forms which it receives.[3]
In one beloved presence, nay and more,   255
In that most apprehensive habitude[4]
And those sensations which have been deriv'd
From this beloved Presence, there exists
A virtue which irradiates and exalts
All objects through all intercourse of sense.   260
No outcast he, bewilder'd and depress'd;
Along his infant veins are interfus'd[5]
The gravitation and the filial bond
Of nature[6] that connect him with the world.[7]
Emphatically such a Being lives,   265
An inmate of this *active* universe;[8]
From nature[9] largely he receives; nor so
Is satisfied, but largely gives again,
For feeling has to him imparted strength,
And powerful in all sentiments of grief,   270

[1] Recognizes its affinity with another human soul.
[2] The baby, in learning to combine sense-impressions into a recognizable image of its mother, has its first experience of creative perception.
[3] 'Tenacious' implies the creative, 'receives' the passive elements of perception.
[4] Readiness to be emotionally out-reaching.
[5] Poured in and absorbed.
[6] Human nature.
[7] Communion with his mother stabilizes the baby emotionally, like gravity.
[8] Wordsworth insists that the mind's relation to the world is dynamic and reciprocal.
[9] Here, the power informing the whole created universe, human and material.

Of exultation, fear, and joy, his mind,
Even as an agent of the one great mind,[1]
Creates, creator and receiver both,
Working but in alliance with the works
Which it beholds.——Such, verily, is the first   275
Poetic[2] spirit of our human life;
By uniform control of after years
In most abated and suppress'd, in some
Through every change of growth or of decay,
Preeminent till death.   280

1798–1805   1926

iii) Waiting for the horses (1805, xi. 345–89)

One Christmas-time,   345
The day before the Holidays began,
Feverish, and tired, and restless, I went forth
Into the fields, impatient for the sight
Of those two Horses which should bear us home,
My brothers and myself. There was a Crag,   350
An Eminence,[3] which from the meeting point
Of two high-ways ascending, overlook'd
At least a long half-mile of those two roads,
By each of which the expected Steeds might come,
The choice uncertain. Thither I repair'd,   355
Up to the highest summit: 'twas a day
Stormy, and rough, and wild, and on the grass
I sate, half shelter'd by a naked wall:
Upon my right hand was a single sheep,
A whistling hawthorn on my left, and there,   360
With those Companions at my side, I watch'd
Straining my eyes intensely, as the mist
Gave intermitting prospect of the wood
And plain beneath. Ere I to School return'd

[1] God.
[2] From Greek *poiein*. to make.
[3] High point in the landscape.

That dreary time, ere I had been ten days 365
A Dweller in my Father's House, he died[1]
And I and my two Brothers, orphans then,[2]
Followed his Body to the Grave. The event,
With all the sorrow which it brought appear'd
A chastisement;[3] and when I call'd to mind 370
That day so lately pass'd, when from the crag
I look'd in such anxiety of hope,
With trite reflections of morality,
Yet in the deepest passion, I bow'd low
To God, who thus corrected my desires; 375
And afterwards, the wind and sleety rain
And all the business of the elements,
The single sheep, and the one blasted tree,
And the bleak music of that old stone wall,
The noise of wood and water, and the mist 380
Which on the line of each of those two Roads
Advanced in such indisputable shapes,[4]
All these were spectacles and sounds to which
I often would repair, and thence would drink
As at a fountain: and I do not doubt 385
That in this later time, when storm and rain
Beat on my roof at midnight, or by day
When I am in the woods, unknown to me
The workings of my spirit thence are brought.

1798–1805   1926

[1] His father, John, died on 30 December 1783, aged 42. Wordsworth was 13.
[2] Their mother having died five years earlier.
[3] Punishment.
[4] Too indefinite to be disputed.

[St Paul's]

Press'd with conflicting thoughts of love and fear,
I parted from thee, Friend![1] and took my way
Through the great City,[2] pacing with an eye
Down cast, ear sleeping, and feet masterless
That were sufficient guide unto themselves,   5
And step by step went pensively. Now, mark!
Not how my trouble was entirely hush'd,
(That might not be) but how, by sudden gift,
Gift of Imagination's holy power,[3]
My Soul in her uneasiness received   10
An anchor of stability. It chanced
That, while I thus was pacing, I raised up
My heavy eyes and instantly beheld,
Saw at a glance in that familiar spot
A visionary[4] scene: a length of street   15
Laid open in its morning quietness,
Deep, hollow, unobstructed, vacant, smooth,
And white with winter's purest white, as fair,
As fresh and spotless as he ever sheds
On field or mountain. Moving Form was none   20
Save here and there a shadowy Passenger,[5]
Slow, shadowy, silent, dusky, and beyond
And high above this winding length of street,
This noiseless and unpeopled avenue,
Pure, silent, solemn, beautiful, was seen   25
The huge majestic Temple of St Paul
In awful sequestration,[6] through a veil,
Through its own sacred veil of falling snow.

1808   1947

---

[1] Coleridge, whom Wordsworth had just visited.
[2] London.
[3] By 'imagination', Wordsworth means the capacity for benignly creative perception.
[4] Having the revelatory quality of a spiritual vision.
[5] Person passing by.
[6] A majestic isolation from the secular world, inspiring awe.